# CHARACTER
# EDUCATION
# BOOK OF PLAYS
## Middle Grade Level

**by Judy Truesdell Mecca**

Incentive Publications, Inc.
Nashville, Tennessee

*Illustrated by Gayle Harvey*
*Cover by Becky Ruegger*
*Edited by Jean K. Signor*

ISBN 0-86530-486-6

PRINTED IN THE UNITED STATES OF AMERICA
www.incentivepublications.com

# Table of Contents

# Overview
# Character Education Book of Plays
# Middle Grade Level

Young people today are faced with more choices than previous generations. We give them house keys and expect them to avoid trouble, even though they are unsupervised. We drop them at the mall and hope they do not make the wrong choices, fall in with the wrong crowd, do something slightly less than moral or even illegal. Many young people attend unchaperoned parties or are even offered illegal substances by parents wishing to be perceived as cool.

As parents, teachers, and group leaders, we try to protect our children; however, every child, must make some decisions daily without adult involvement, especially as they embark on the middle school and high school journey. We hope that we have taught them well, and that we have armed them with common sense and the moral compass they need to make the right choices.

For many students, it is more fun to get up and perform than it is to write a report or read a book about a topic. With many Americans feeling less optimistic about the character development of our children, it is incumbent upon us to use every available tool.

This collection of monologues, duets, short plays, and one two-act play encourages such issues as respect, love, honesty, responsibility, commitment, courage, patience, joyfulness, tolerance, loyalty, and citizenship in a fun, hopeful, and often humorous way. These scenes will be fun to perform, not only in Theatre Arts class, but in other classes, scout meetings, church groups, or the recreation center. As an added attraction, many children who would not thrive in a traditional academic environment may shine when they perform on stage. Theatre combines communication, creativity, and self-expression, often resulting in amazing surprises.

As with all of Incentive Publication's play collections, suggestions for scenery, costumes, and props are included, as well as classroom exercises and discussion topics relative to the values with the plays.

Have a good time! Make programs! Rig up makeshift costumes! Cut mustaches out of construction paper and throw popcorn! Do not worry about the character education—that will be sneaking in between the lines.

# We Want Respect

## A Boy Band song about Respect

# We Want Respect

## A Boy Band song to the tune of
### *I Want You Back* by NSync

It's something that we all want

It's something that we all need, yeah

So tell me what to do now, 'cause

I, I, I, I, I, I

Want respect


It's hard to say I'm sorry

When I treat my brother hatefully

A lesson I've learned too well for sure
    (ahhh-ah-ah-ah)

But just give us a listen

We're trying to figure out just what to do

And we're gonna share some thoughts with you

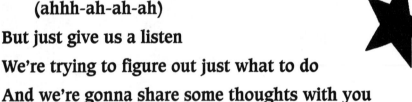

It's something that we all want

It's something that we all need, yeah

We'll tell you what to do now

When you want respect

First and most important

We must feel respect for ourselves inside

Respect for where we came from, where we started
    (ahhh-ah-ah-ah)

If your parents told you
"Stand tall and everything will be all right!"
I'm telling you now that they were right!
Now take care of your body
(Baby) You're only gonna get one
So keep the drugs and booze out
Show yourself respect

We want respect—Uh huh—Yeah

Let the friends you want
Be the friends you need
Babe, hang with the best

Keep an eye up high
Where the good things are
That is what we should do

It's something that your friends want
And even Mom and Dad need
You know, even *Mr. Payne, now
They all want respect

It's something that we all want
It's something that we all need
Respect the world around you
And you'll get respect!

*(*Insert the name of your principal or appropriate teacher here)*

*Character Education Book of Plays*
*Middle Grade Level*

# The Love Confusion
## A Game Show Play
## About Love

*Character Education Book of Plays*
*Middle Grade Level*

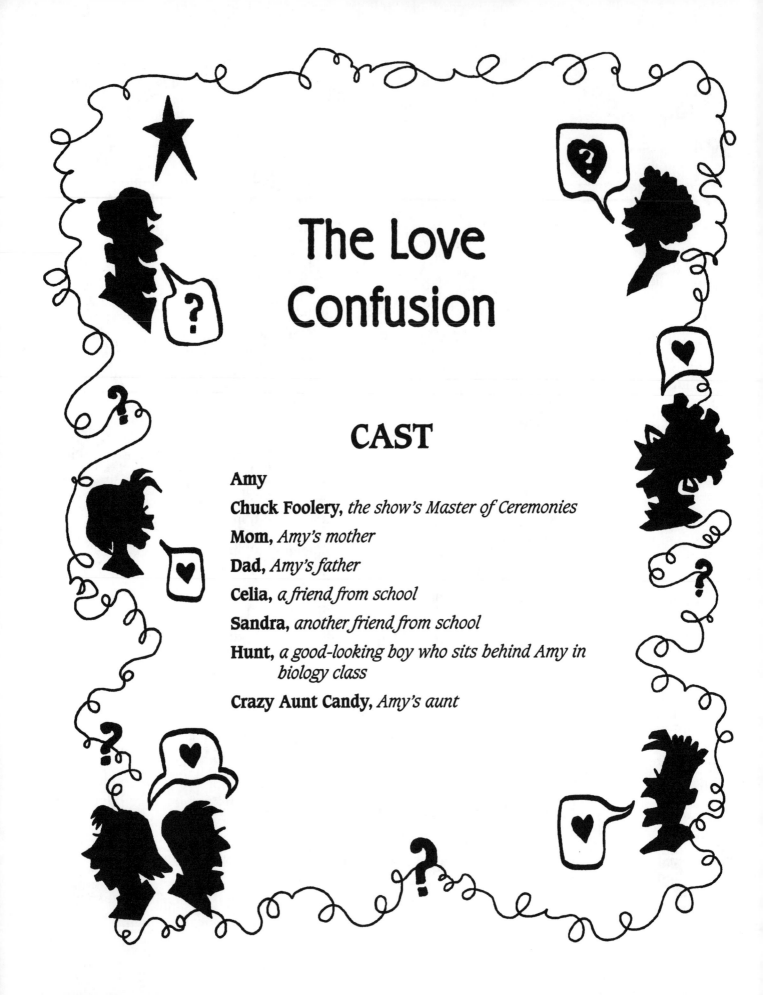

# The Love Confusion

## CAST

**Amy**

**Chuck Foolery,** *the show's Master of Ceremonies*

**Mom,** *Amy's mother*

**Dad,** *Amy's father*

**Celia,** *a friend from school*

**Sandra,** *another friend from school*

**Hunt,** *a good-looking boy who sits behind Amy in biology class*

**Crazy Aunt Candy,** *Amy's aunt*

# The Love Confusion

## Notes to the Teacher/Director

Love, love love! It's mentioned in the lyrics of every song on the radio (especially when your heart has just been broken). Every perfume promises to bring love. Even advertisements for unlikely products such as cars seem to imply that the right car will deliver the right handsome man or beautiful woman to your door like the morning paper.

So, no wonder we are all confused. Is love something you can get out of a lip gloss tube or a new convertible? Is it something we go out and find or something that just drops on us from above? When is it real and when it is an illusion?

*The Love Confusion* is a humorous play using the game-show format, borrowed from *The Dating Game* and *The Love Connection*, either of which you may have seen in television re-runs. Our "love queen" for the day, Amy, is asking questions to mystery contestants on the other side of a screen, trying to determine who really loves her the most.

In real life (if we're lucky) many people love us in many different ways. This play deals with some ways which are not so genuine, such as people who love us because of what we can do for them in return, or to try to re-create us in their own image. Or because we're cute. (Granted, that's good for a start—but lots more goes into actually loving someone than just finding a nice-looking outer package.) What kind of love is real? Who really loves Amy for the right reasons?

*Character Education Book of Plays*
*Middle Grade Level*

# ⟨♥?♥⟩ The Love Confusion

## Scenery

Scenically, all you'll need to produce this play in class or on a stage will be a screen and five stools. (You could also use regular chairs, but stools will make your actors a little higher and easier to see.)
For the screen, you can pinch a big piece of cardboard between two chairs or hang it from the ceiling or build a free-standing divider out of wood. You could hang a bedspread from a wire stretched across your classroom. (Remember—it's a low-budget show.)

"Corny '60s game show music" is mentioned in a couple of places in the script. If you can tape this off of re-run television, that would be great. Most anything by the group Tijuana Brass should work just fine. You can also look at the record shop—sometimes you can find collections of game show music. Whatever you choose, record it on a tape player and have a stage hand press the button at the appropriate times. If the music can't be found, just remove the lines referring to the music. (Or, you could have an a cappella choir or singers humming some tune off stage.)

## Costumes

Amy and Sandra should wear normal school clothes, but Celia needs to look as if she took a great deal of care getting ready for the camera. Lots of make-up—the latest fashion—she's always got one eye to her mental mirror. You might age Mom and Dad a little bit with baby powder temples and/or glasses, and choose age-appropriate clothing for them. Chuck Foolery can wear a bad-taste jacket—maybe even one with a '60s look to it, in keeping with our "corny '60s" theme. Wildest of all will be Crazy Aunt Candy, who should be outrageous in huge earrings, bright colors, maybe a feather boa or sequined jacket, and sunglasses—nothing is too much for this wild woman.

# The Love Confusion

## Teaching Materials to Accompany *The Love Confusion*

1. Write a short paper about a person who really loves you. How do you know he or she loves you? What is your evidence? Do you know only by the things he or she says, or do his or her actions let you know also? What are they? Does this person always agree with your ideas?
   How do you act in return?

2. As a class, discuss things that demonstrate love which may not seem to be. For instance, taking good care of a pet shows your love for it. If your family doctor gives you a call to see if the medicine he prescribed is working, is that a kind of love? How about when your parents say no to something they think might be dangerous, even if you want to do it? Is that love or are they just being mean?

3. Take two of the characters out of the play and put them in another location. For instance, take Celia and Amy and put them . . . where? In a veterinarian's office? Running into each other at the mall? Alongside the road where their cars have just crashed into each other? .....Now improvise a scene. How do they act? How would they speak to each other? How would each respond to the situation? Here are some other interesting combinations—or you can create your own.
   - Dad and Chuck Foolery in a dental office waiting room
   - Crazy Aunt Candy and Mom trying on clothes at a sale
   - Hunt and Celia at a rock concert
   - Sandra and Hunt forced to work together on a project, such as dissecting a frog

4. For the rest of the day, notice ways different people have of demonstrating their love for you and for each other.
   Write a brief paper or journal entry about what you observe.

# The Love Confusion

## A Game Show Play
## About Love

*(As the play begins, we see AMY sitting on a stool on one side of a screen. On the other side, out of AMY's sight, are seated MOM and DAD; SANDRA and CELIA (two of AMY's friends); HUNT (a good-looking guy who sits behind AMY in Biology class; and CRAZY AUNT CANDY, AMY's nutty aunt). MOM and DAD are trying hard to share one stool, as though they are a team. The rest of the contestants have their own stools, and are spaced apart evenly. Everyone is chatting softly, as they wait for the show to begin.)*

*(Corny game show music from the '60s plays as our host, CHUCK FOOLERY, enters, running excitedly and waving to the audience and contestants. The music fades as he speaks from center stage.)*

| | |
|---|---|
| **Chuck Foolery** | Good evening or morning, whichever it is, ladies and gentlemen, and welcome to The Love Confusion! I'm your host, Chuck Foolery . . . |
| **Everyone on Stage** | Hi, Chuck! |
| **Chuck Foolery** | Wo! Was that rehearsed? Who knows! Anyway, let's get started with today's LOVELY episode of The Love Confusion! Let's meet our love queen for the day—Amy! *(crosses over to her)* Hello, Amy! |
| **Amy** | Hello Chuck! I'm a little nervous! |
| **Chuck Foolery** | Just a little? You oughta be a lot nervous! Look out there at all those people! *(AMY looks at the audience, with a terrified look on her face)* Just kidding, Amy, just kidding! Now, tell us a little about yourself. Where do you go to school? |

*Character Education Book of Plays*
*Middle Grade Level*

# The Love Confusion

**Amy**     I'm a Junior at McBeal High School! Go Alley Cats!

**Chuck Foolery**     All right, Amy, you've obviously got a lot of school spirit. But we're here today to see if we can solve a mystery in your life!

**Amy**     Is this going to be about the cafeteria food?

**Chuck Foolery**     Do me a favor, Ames, leave the jokes to me, what do ya say? Now, we're going to see if we can solve the mystery of who loves Amy the most! There are several contestants on the other side of the screen, Amy, all of whom claim that they love you. You're going to ask them questions and see if you can decide who really loves you and has your best interest at heart!

**Amy**     Sounds like fun!

**Chuck Foolery**     I certainly hope so, or we're going to have some disappointed sponsors. OK, Amy—we're going to introduce the contestants to the audience, so you need to disappear into our soundproof booth.

**Amy**     See ya later! *(she exits)*

**Chuck Foolery**     *(crossing to MOM and DAD, who are still trying to fit on one stool)* Contestants number one are Amy's Mom and Dad! Let's hear it for them! *(everyone applauds)*

**Mom**     Thanks for letting us share a spot, Chuck!

**Dad**     We really are a team where Amy is concerned!

**Mom**     That's right. She's our daughter and . . .

# The Love Confusion

**Dad**     We love her!

**Chuck Foolery**     I know you do!

**Mom**     Chuck, there's one thing . . . do you think we could have another stool?

**Dad**     It's a little hard to share one . . .

**Chuck Foolery**     Sorry, folks, low budget show. Good luck to you—we know you love your daughter!

*(MOM and DAD smile weakly as they struggle to fit on the same stool. DAD finally gives up and stands behind MOM as CHUCK FOOLERY moves on to CELIA.)*

**Chuck Foolery**     Ladies and gentlemen, please say hello to Amy's friend from school, Celia!

*(Applause)*

**Celia**     Oh, my gosh, I am SO not believing that I am actually on television! This is SO exciting—how do I look? Does my hair look bouncy—do my teeth look white—is my forehead shiny?

**Chuck Foolery**     Hold still, Celia, let me use your forehead as a mirror to check my own hair! *(pretends to be seeing his reflection in CELIA's forehead)*

**Celia**     Chuck, you get out of here! You are so bad!

*(waving to imaginary camera)* Hi, everybody from McBeal High School—I love you all! Do you love me!

*(back to Chuck)* Do I look OK, really? You never did say.

**Chuck Foolery**     Celia, you look just as good as . . . you are inside.

# The Love Confusion

| | |
|---|---|
| **Celia** | That is SO sweet of you to say! *(realizing that CHUCK may not exactly have paid her a compliment)* Hey wait . . . |
| **Chuck Foolery** | Moving right along, please welcome Amy's friend since kindergarten, Sandra! |

*(Applause)*

| | |
|---|---|
| **Sandra** | Hi, everybody! |
| **Chuck Foolery** | Hello, Sandra, and how are you? |
| **Sandra** | Oh, I'm fine. I just hope Amy has a good time today. |
| **Celia** | Say, are there prizes? Do we, like you know, win anything if she picks us? |
| **Chuck Foolery** | Celia—would you do something for me? Press your lips together and make sure your lipstick is even. *(She presses her lips together, then gets angry and pouts as she realizes she's been tricked into being quiet.)* So Sandra—you and Amy have been friends since kindergarten? |
| **Sandra** | That's right. A mean boy was picking on her on the playground and I went and punched him in the nose. We've been best friends ever since. |
| **Chuck Foolery** | Oooh, sounds like *(singing)* "Everybody was Kung Fu fighting!" |
| **Sandra** | Yeah, I guess . . . |
| **Chuck Foolery** | OK, well, good luck to you today—let's hope she picks you as the one who loves her the most! |
| **Sandra** | I do love her—she's my best friend. |

# The Love Confusion

**Chuck Foolery**  Our next contestant is a young man . . .

**Celia**  He's a total babe, and I am not kidding.

**Chuck Foolery**  I stand corrected! This "babe" sits behind Amy in Biology class at school. Please put your hands together for Hunt!

*(As everyone applauds, HUNT puts his hands together in front of him and looks confused.)*

So, Hunt, I know you sit by Amy in Biology class, but is there any Chemistry between you?

**Hunt**  *(cluelessly, in a daze)* Uh . . . what?

**Chuck Foolery**  Forget it kid, just making a joke.

*(aside, to audience)* Some days are harder than others.

*(speaking to HUNT again)* So, Hunt, do you like to?

**Hunt**  Do I like to what?

**Chuck Foolery**  To "hunt." Get it? That's your name—so I was wondering . . .

**Hunt**  What?

**Chuck Foolery**  You know—never mind. Good luck in today's game.

**Hunt**  What?

**Chuck Foolery**  *(crossing to CRAZY AUNT CANDY)* Last but not least, Amy's favorite aunt, Crazy Aunt Candy!

*(Applause)*

# The Love Confusion

**Crazy Aunt Candy**  Well, hello, Chuck, it's certainly a pleasure to be on television with such a handsome and charming host. I was just saying to my husband . . . well, you know, if I actually HAD a husband, which I don't . . . but if I did, I would just say to him "I wish you were good looking like Chuck Foolery!" I bet he wouldn't like that much more than a roach likes Raid, what do ya bet?!

**Dad**  Er . . . excuse me, Chuck? I just want to say that this is my little sister, but she's . . . well, she's just a little bit . . . different, if you know what I mean.

**Mom**  She marches to a different drummer, that's for sure!

**Chuck**  If you ask me, she marches to a drummer on the planet Mars. But thanks for the warning. So, Crazy Aunt Candy . . .

**Crazy Aunt Candy**  You don't have to call me that whole long name, Chuck! That's just what my family calls me. I mean, I think of you as family, just from this short time we've been talking. I feel that we're really close. But no, you can just call me . . . let's see . . . how about Crazy? Yeah, just call me Crazy if you want to. Most people just call me Candy, but I feel wild being here on television today, so I think I'd rather be called Crazy. How about it?

**Chuck**  I will have no trouble in the world calling you "Crazy;" you can count on that.
*(addressing the audience)* Well, you can call me crazy, but I think it's time to bring Amy out here to begin the game! Amy, come on back!

*(AMY re-enters, smiling and ready to begin to play. She has several note cards with her, on which questions are printed.)*

# The Love Confusion

**Chuck**   All right, Amy, I see that you have your questions ready.

**Amy**   Yes, they're all written out on these notecards!

**Chuck**   Great! Now—you'll ask your questions to the contestants on the other side of this voice-altering screen.

**Amy**   Voice-altering?

**Chuck**   Yes, Amy. Since you would probably recognize the voices of the contestants, we've built that screen which will alter their voices slightly so you won't recognize them.

**Amy**   Never heard of that before!

**Chuck**   This is an extremely cutting-edge show, Amy.
*(toward MOM and DAD)* And that's why we can't afford a million extra stools!

*(MOM and DAD nod understandingly and CHUCK addresses AMY again.)* Now, ready to get started?

*(she nods)* Well, let's begin. Ask your first question . . . now!

**Amy**   Contestant Number 1 . . .

**Mom and Dad**   *(speaking at the same time, but not necessarily in unison)* Yes, dear? We're right here!

**Amy**   For English class, I have to write a report on another country. I have two weeks until it's due. What do I do now?

**Mom**   May I?

**Dad**   Take it away!

# ♥?♥ The Love Confusion

**Mom**  Sweetheart, you use your home computer—if you have one—to look up information about that country. You compile all your facts in a well-organized way and write a rough draft of your report. You get someone to read it . . .

**Dad**  Like perhaps your mother or father . . .

**Mom**  *(whacking her husband playfully on the arm and shushing him, not wanting him to give them away)* And then you touch it up, type it up neatly, and hand it in a week early.

**Dad**  Maybe your teacher will give you extra credit!

**Mom**  Maybe, but even if she doesn't, Amy will have the project over with and off of her mind so she can enjoy the next couple of weeks without anything hanging over her head.

**Amy**  Thanks . . . that sounds like good advice . . . and strangely familiar . . . oh well . . . same question, Contestant Number 2?

**Celia**  Oh my gosh, well . . . first, you start thinking of excuses about why you can't do the report at all. You go up to the teacher after class and ask her some bogus question, but make sure to sniffle and get a tissue so she thinks you're coming down with a cold or something? If you can sneeze, that's even better. Then skip class the next day, so when the report comes due, you can say you've been too sick to do any work and you're really behind. Maybe she'll forget about it all together. You could also say someone in your family passed away and you had to go out of town to the funeral. Or—oh, I like this better—you could say you couldn't think of any country to write a report about.

# The Love Confusion

**Amy**  But what about my grades?

**Celia**  Well—you know, no pain no gain.

**Amy**  Uh, huh. What do you think, Contestant Number 3?

**Sandra**  I pretty much think the same thing as your . . . as Contestants Number 1. Write it—get it over with. I would add that sometimes when you write a report about a country or some place you don't know about, it's fun to learn new stuff about that place.

**Celia**  *(sarcastically)* Oh, I am so sure.

**Sandra**  Let me say it in your language, Contestant Number 2. You know when a new make-up counter opens at the mall and you visit it for the first time?

**Celia**  And there are all those new colors to choose from and new kinds of mascara? And maybe even a free gift?

**Sandra**  Yes! And you didn't know about that place to buy cosmetics before—but now you do! You learned something new!

**Celia**  Oh my gosh, now I see! I think . . .

**Chuck**  Amy, let's have your next question, please.

**Amy**  OK. I think I want to ask the same question to Contestant Number 4, please, Chuck.

**Hunt**  What?

**Amy**  What do I do about my report that's due in two weeks?

**Hunt**  What?

# The Love Confusion

**Amy**    What do I . . . oh never mind.

**Celia**    He is the cutest babe in the school, I'm not kidding.

**Amy**    I'll skip to Contestant Number 5. Number 5? My report?

**Crazy Aunt Candy**    Well, girlfriend, the first thing I would do is hop on a plane and fly to the country that you have to write your report about. Buy all new clothes and maybe new luggage *(Amy's parents shake their heads and seem to be getting headaches.)* Then when you're there, dress like the people who live there, eat in their restaurants, see what life is like there! I remember one time I went away to art school in Bora-Bora . . . or was it Indonesia?

**Dad**    It was Austin *(or insert the name of a local town)*. You just went away to college.

**Crazy Aunt Candy**    No, I'm thinking about another time! I worked as a waitress in a little bistro alongside the French Riviera . . .

**Dad**    McDonald's. The only thing French about your job was the fries.

**Crazy Aunt Candy**    You are just misrepresenting my life, Contestant Number 1!
I lived the life of an artist and drew sketches of people riding by on their camels and rickshaws—and then . . . I . . . came home and wrote a report about it for school. That's what I think you should do.

**Amy**    Thanks . . . Contestant Number 5. OK, here's my next question. I'm at a party, and some kids bring out some beer. What do I do? Contestant Number . . . 2.

# The Love Confusion

**Celia**  Well . . . I know beer isn't really good for you or anything . . . but if you say no to it, some people will like laugh at you and think you're a real, you know, nerd? So I say go ahead and drink one or two, just be sure to brush your teeth or chew gum before you go home.

**Sandra**  Oh, hold on, I disagree. I knew you would say something like that Ce . . . Number 2. If you go along with everything everybody suggests, you're not you're own person at all! You're just one of the sheep being herded along with the rest of the pack, or whatever sheep travel in. You just said beer isn't good for you . . .

**Celia**  Well, I know it can make you FAT, for one thing, oh my gosh . . .

**Sandra**  Right, it can at least make you fat. So if you know that, why wouldn't you just say "No, thank you!"? If those people are going to think you're a nerd or whatever, you don't need them anyway. They're just . . . drunk sheep.

**Amy**  Interesting answers, Numbers 2 and 3. Was that Number 3?

**Sandra**  Yes, I'm Number 3. And boy, are you right about her—she's really "Number 2."

**Celia**  Hey . . . was I just insulted?

**Amy**  What do you think, Number 1? Do I have a beer?

*(MOM appears to have fainted onto DAD)*

*Character Education Book of Plays*
*Middle Grade Level*

# The Love Confusion

**Dad**     Well, my partner here is feeling a little ill, so I'll answer. Here it is. Here's my answer. There is nothing good that can come of drinking alcohol. You may feel good for a few minutes, but then you feel worse than when you started. You act stupid, you fall around, and you put yourself in danger if you try to drive a car. And if you ever get in the car with anyone who has been drinking, I'll ground you for the rest of your life. I mean . . . that is . . . you could really be hurt. There's just no reason to start. Oh, and you'll have bad breath.

**Amy**     Ew! Contestant Number 4? What about beer?

**Hunt**     *(perking up a little)* Beer? All right!

**Sandra**     See? Do you want to be like that loser?

**Celia**     Loser? He's like the coolest babe in school . . .

**Hunt**     What?

**Amy**     And what do you say about me having a brew, Contestant Number 5?

**Crazy Aunt Candy**     I would advise you to ask for a fine bottle of wine, instead. Maybe a lovely little Merlot, light, yet frisky. And you look so graceful holding a wine glass. Why, once when I was in Paris for a fashion show . . .

*(MOM has come to briefly, then faints again hearing CRAZY AUNT CANDY advising AMY to drink wine.)*

**Dad**     Stop giving bad advice . . . er . . . Contestant 5! You don't drink wine—you're allergic to it and it makes you break out in hives!

**Crazy Aunt Candy**     That is just not true. It gives me a blush like a rose . . .

# The Love Confusion

**Dad**   I give up.

*(corny '60s game show music plays again.)*

**Chuck Foolery**   Oops! I hear that corny game show music from the '60s, letting us know that it's time for you to make a decision, Amy!

**Amy**   Chuck, it's hard to decide. Could each one of the contestants give me a final comment?

**Chuck Foolery**   Yes, but they should all be brief—we are almost out of time!

**Amy**   Contestants Number 1?

**Chuck Foolery**   Closing remarks, please.

**Dad**   I just want to say that, though my partner and I may seem like we have a lot of rules, or pester Amy to live up to her obligations . . .

**Mom**   It's just that we really love her with all our hearts. We would never have another happy day if anything happened to her—and, well, we're going to nag and scold her until we make sure she is all grown up and safe.

**Dad**   And the kind of woman we know she can be.

**Amy**   Thanks, that's a good answer. Number 2?

**Celia**   Oh . . . what? I wasn't paying attention for a minute.

**Chuck Foolery**   Why do you love Amy, Number 2?

# The Love Confusion

**Celia**  Well—the real truth is—I love everybody. I mean, well you know, everybody who can vote for me when I run for stuff at school. Like Homecoming Queen or Junior Class Favorite? I have my dress all picked out for Homecoming Queen, you know, just in case. It's blue—like my eyes—no, I'm just kidding. Anyway, sure I love Amy. And I really love being on television. Hello everybody at McBeal! I love you all!

**Sandra**  If I could just interrupt this paid political announcement—Amy is someone who just makes you love her. She's nice, she cares about helping other people, she doesn't collect up friends like they were trophies she could put in a case. I have cared about her since . . . well, for a long time for one reason: she is lovable. I've had fun today, Chuck. Thanks for letting me come on the show.

**Chuck Foolery**  Thank you, Number 3.

**Crazy Aunt Candy**  Excuse me, Chuck? Can I take my turn? I don't want to wait. *(not waiting for a reply, just rattling on)* I just want to say that I think Amy should enjoy life to the fullest, no matter what she has to spend or what damage she does to herself. Life is a roller coaster ride! I want her to be as much like me as she possibly can be. There—that's how much I love that young lady!

**Chuck Foolery**  Er . . . thank you, Contestant Number 5. Moving on . . . Number 4? Final remarks for Amy?

**Hunt**  What?

**Amy**  Number 4, what's your final answer? Do ya love me or not?

# The Love Confusion

**Hunt**  I have loved you since the moment your sun began to shine across my airspace. You are like the dew on the morning grass, reflecting sparkles of joy for all to see. There are not words to describe my love for you, except a few, like endless, overpowering, all-encompassing, and eternal. You are the sun; you are the moon; you are the stars that haven't gone supernova yet. I need sunglasses even to look at your radiance.

*(AMY looks like she might swoon off of her stool.)*

**Chuck Foolery**  That was surprising, coming from you, Number 4. Is that your own composition?

**Hunt**  Oh no, man, it's from the new CD by the Pierced Navels. The real truth is—I just like girls.

**Amy**  Do you even know me, Number 4?

**Hunt**  What?

**Chuck Foolery**  OK, Amy, now we really are out of time—thank heavens! So—who do you pick as the contestant who loves you the most?

**Amy**  Well, it's really hard, Chuck, because believe it or not, I think every one of the contestants does care about me in some way. But let me rule them out one by one. First, the contestant who loves me only because I'm a girl and therefore someone who might worship him—I did not pick Contestant Number 4!

**Hunt**  *(rising and coming around the screen to shake hands with AMY)* Hey—don't you sit in front of me in Biology? *(exits)*

*Character Education Book of Plays*
*Middle Grade Level*

# The Love Confusion

**Chuck Foolery**   Thanks for playing, Hunt, and bye bye. Who else did you rule out, Amy?

**Amy**   Well—there is one contestant who seems to love me only because of what I could do for her, and I don't think that's real caring. True friends love each other and try to help each other—they don't just want to be voted for. So—sorry Number 2—I didn't pick you.

**Celia**   *(crossing over to AMY's side of the screen)* Hi, Amy, can you believe it's me, Celia?! I bet you're surprised. Anyway, it's OK you didn't pick me—at least I got to be on television and now I'll probably get to do commercials, or something. See? Look how good I'll be: *(to audience)* Do you have hair that just won't fluff? I used to, until I started using Flat-No-More, the dryer sheets for hair! Just one on your pillow . . .

**Chuck Foolery**   I'm sure the network will be in touch, Celia. But bye for now!

**Celia**   Bye, Chuck! Bye everybody! Remember—vote Celia for . . . whatever! *(exits)*

**Chuck Foolery**   Well, we're down to only three contestants, Amy. Whom will you rule out next?

**Amy**   Well, Chuck—sometimes I think grown-ups make a mistake. They want us kids to live our lives like they didn't get to. Sometimes they buy us expensive stuff that they couldn't afford when they were kids—or they want us to live wild, exciting lives because they didn't get to. I really think a certain contestant does love me—but she's thinking more about herself than me. So I have to say good-bye to Contestant Number 5.

# The Love Confusion

**Crazy Aunt Candy** *(coming around the screen)* Amy, you are just nuts. I do live an exciting wild life and I just want you to join in! Be like me—ride elephants in Africa, meet tall dark handsome strangers on the banks of various rivers!

**Amy** Good-bye, Crazy Aunt Candy.

**Crazy Aunt Candy** *(as she exits)* Good-bye, one and all! Forward my mail to the Savannah!

**Amy** Now, Chuck—this is hard. Contestants Number 1 obviously love me and would put my safety and well being ahead of their own. But Contestant Number 3 loves me because she met me and decided I was worth loving. So believe it or not—I have to declare a tie between Numbers 1 and 3!

**Chuck Foolery** Mom, Dad, Sandra—come on around!

**Dad** You know how much I love you, sweetie.

**Mom** You are my heart.

**Sandra** Good choice, Amy my old friend! Any playground bullies I need to beat up for you?

*(AMY and the winning contestants link arms affectionately. CELIA, HUNT and CRAZY AUNT CANDY re-enter together on their side of the screen. CELIA and CRAZY AUNT CANDY are obviously flirting with HUNT.)*

**Chuck Foolery** I'd love to hear the answer to that one, but we're out of time! Tune in tomorrow—until then, we wish you all luck, happiness, and most of all . . .

**Cast** *(blows a big kiss to the audience, then says in unison:)* LOVE!

*(All wave good-bye as, once again, corny '60s game show music plays)*

*Character Education Book of Plays*
*Middle Grade Level*

# The Same But Different

## A Play About Tolerance

# The Same But Different

## CAST

**Connor Sherwood**

**Mom,** *Connor's mom*

**Jason Yeager**

**Cassie Yeager,** *Jason's sister*

**Eddie Welch,** *a man at the convention*

**Convention participants**

# The Same But Different

## Notes to the Teacher/Director

"She's taller than me!"

"We're different colors!"

"He's a lot richer—look at the clothes he wears to school!"

We can't help but notice and think about differences which we perceive in people we meet. It's natural. Some differences are obvious, such as race, size and sex. (Even animals decide whether to approach each other based on appearance, a practice which sometimes saves their lives!) Some differences are more subtle, and not obvious on the surface, such as religion and values.

The dictionary definition of tolerance is "The capacity for or the practice of recognizing and respecting the opinions, practices and behavior of others." Should it end there, or should we also recognize and respect physical differences which may seem daunting at first?

In the play *The Same But Different*, two boys meet on the Internet because they have a very specific interest in common—The War Between the States or, as it is more commonly called, The Civil War. One boy, Jason, is wheelchair-bound, a fact of which his new friend Connor is not aware. They make plans to meet at a convention of Civil War enthusiasts, which concerns Jason's sister. She is afraid Connor may have some expectations which Jason may not be able to meet because of his limitation. Jason decides to take the risk. When the boys do meet, the strength of their common interest completely overwhelms the physical difference of the wheelchair. Saying "Let's roll!" Connor wheels Jason off to the first exhibit, and we have the sense that a lifelong friendship has formed despite a very obvious difference. What the boys have in common is stronger than what makes them different.

## Props and Scenery

To produce this play, you will need to create the illusion of two boys typing at two computers in different cities. Of course, you can set up keyboards and monitors, making sure that they are angled so as not to block your actors' faces. You could also pantomime the monitor, with lots of pointing and indicating, and have the actual keyboard on stage—or you could pantomime both computers entirely.

The dialogue makes it clear that computers are being used. If you have access to stage lighting, light the area of the stage featuring the boy who is in the scene at the time, "blacking out" the other boy's area, then switch the lights as the focus of the play changes.

If you do not have a boy available to play the role of Jason, who is actually in a wheelchair, borrow a chair from the school clinic, local hospital, or nursing home.

Computer technology changes every day. At the time of this publication, **America Online** provides a service called "Instant Messenger" which the boys use in order to communicate. If a different, more widely-recognized instant communication service is available when this play is produced, feel free to change the name.

## Costumes

Regarding costumes, Connor, Jason, and Cassie wear normal clothes, with the exception of Connor's red rose. You may wish to age Mom a little by costume or make-up. The real challenge will be the participants at the Civil War conference. If one or two authentic uniforms could be rented from a local costume house, that would be ideal. Otherwise, (or in addition) use the Internet or books to research the uniforms of the infantrymen of the time and use your imagination to simulate them (just as the folks coming to the convention would). You may wish to fashion a rifle musket out of foam or paper maché; again, research the appearance of this unique weapon on-line or at the library.

# THE SAME BUT DIFFERENT

## Teaching Materials to Accompany *The Same But Different*

1. Over the Internet, we are able to make friends in a unique way—we tell them only what we want them to know. They don't have to see us—we don't even have to tell the truth. Is this good? Can it be harmful? As a class, discuss the positive result of this anonymous interaction in the play. Then discuss harmful situations which could arise in real life.

2. The characters Connor and Mom are shown teasing and interacting sarcastically with each other. Are they showing each other disrespect or affection? Discuss the fine line between humorous interaction and insulting behavior. Is there someone in your life who crosses this line? How might he or she change his or her behavior?

3. Write a short paper describing a situation in which your first impression of a person (based on his or her appearance) proved to be incorrect as you became better acquainted. It need not be similar to the experiences of the characters in the play—maybe someone who was attractive actually had a rather UNattractive personality.

4. The War Between the States was a complex war which affected the United States of America in numerous ways. Individually, in pairs, or as a group, you may wish to research this time in the history of our young country and prepare an art project, speech, or other kind of presentation. Here are some suggestions, but feel free to think of your own.

   • What is meant by the term "King Cotton"? How did this contribute to the War Between the States?

   • How did the railroad affect the outcome of the war?

   • Compare the industrial society of the North with the agricultural society of the South, and discuss how these differences led to war.
   (Notice—the American people of the time let their differences overshadow the things they had in common.)

 • How did the election of Abraham Lincoln ignite the tension leading to war?

• Write a monologue in the character of Abe Lincoln. It could be before the war, during, or on his way to the theatre the night he was assassinated.

• Write a letter from Lincoln to a loved one, describing his feelings at one of the above points in history.

• At the time of the Civil War, Americans tended to feel more allegiance to their states than the country. In fact, they viewed the United States of America as a voluntary alliance out of which any state could secede at any time. How would things be different in modern day America if this were still the case? Think in terms of economics, defense, and politics in general.

 • *Uncle Tom's Cabin* by Harriet Beecher Stowe was a novel which was published in the newspaper in 1851 in serial form—that is, a portion at a time. It was later published in its entirety as a book. This anti-slavery piece of literature further inflamed the nation toward war. How would you feel if a piece of creative writing you generated had such an affect on America—or even your school or town? Write a monologue as though you were Ms. Stowe—how would she react to this profound impact? Would she be proud? Guilty? What might the sequel, or follow-up book, be like? What might she write about if she were alive today?

# A Play About
# Tolerance

*(The play begins with CONNOR sitting at a computer stage left. He is typing away, when his mother enters.)*

**Mom** *(sarcastically)* Connor! You're at the computer! I think I'm going to have a heart attack, I'm so surprised!

**Connor** *(looking up)* Very funny, Mom. Would you rather I was out with some street gang? Writing on the sides of buildings? Setting fire to public property?

**Mom** Yes, Connor. Why can't you be like other boys?

**Connor** I'll try to do better. Listen, Mom, seriously—I'm so excited about this guy I've met on-line! Well, I mean, sorta met. I'm going to talk to him later, I hope. See, he has the best Web site I've ever seen about . . .

**Mom** Don't tell me, let me guess. About . . . could it be . . . The Civil War?

**Connor** Excuse me, Mother, I think you mean "The War Between the States", to be more correct?

**Mom** I'm so sorry. But, really? A boy has a Web site about the Civil . . . The War Between the States? There's another boy in America who's as interested in the Civil War as you are?

**Connor** It's not weird! It's fascinating! General Beauregard, "Stonewall" Jackson, Robert E. Lee—I can't help it, I just love it.

**Mom** I know you do, and I think it's great. You know I'm only kidding, don't you when I give you a hard time?

**Connor** Yes, Mom, of course. I know that you think I'm a real brilliant kid because I know about historical events like the Battle of Five Forks.

**Mom** The Battle of Five Forks . . . isn't that the fight over which fork to use for your salad? Led by General Martha Stewart?

**Connor** *(turning back to the computer)* Led by who?

**Mom** Led by whom . . . uh oh, I've lost him! He's got his computer face on again!

**Connor** Mom! The kid with the Web site is on-line! I emailed him and told him how cool I thought his site was, and he sent me his Instant Messenger screen name! So we're about to talk! *(typing and speaking the lines at the same time)* Hello, . . . "Ironsides." Thanks . . . for . . . your . . . screen . . . name. It's . . . great . . . to . . . talk . . . to . . . you!

**Mom** *(as she exits)* Oh well . . . I had my three minutes of quality time with my son . . . into the kitchen where I belong!

*(As MOM exits, JASON enters stage right. He is in a wheelchair. He approaches his computer, and begins to type, speaking the words as he types them.)*

**Jason** Hello . . . Appomattox! Thanks . . . for . . . the . . . good . . . words . . . about . . . my . . . web . . . site! You must be a fan of The War Between the States, too.

*(As the boys talk on-line, we see them type and hear their words. In between, they appear to be reading the response of the other boy on the screen.)*

**Connor** Who isn't? Well, except most people.

*Character Education Book of Plays*
*Middle Grade Level*

44

# The Same But Different

**Jason**  I know what you mean. Not that many of my friends have it as a hobby, but who cares? I'm really interested in everything about the war.

**Connor**  I really am, too! Do you collect miniature soldiers?

**Jason**  I have several sets representing various battles . . . *(JASON's sister CASSIE enters.)* Back in a minute—my sister has invaded my space.

**Cassie**  Jason, I really need to use the computer. I have to look up a current event for Advanced Social Problems tomorrow!

**Jason**  Cassie, you are an advanced social problem! Just look in the mirror and draw a sketch!

**Cassie**  How did I get so lucky to have SUCH a hilarious brother? Shove over, pal—surrender the keyboard.

**Jason**  Well, wait just a minute . . . *(typing again)* My frontal lobotomy candidate sister needs the computer, so I guess I'll talk to you later. I'll probably be back on in a couple of hours.

**Connor**  Nothing good can come of having a sister, that's for sure. Before you sign off, though, I want to let you know about something in my town. I don't know if you're anywhere near *(insert name of hometown here)* but every year about this time there's this whole War Between the States convention here. People dress up in authentic uniforms and re-enact some of the battles. They bring memorabilia and books and stuff to trade—it's great. Anyway, it's coming up in a couple of weeks—do you think you could come?

**Jason**  That sounds great! And I'm not that far away. Maybe my stupid worthless . . . I mean, my beautiful, talented sister with a driver's license will bring me!

**Cassie**   Bring you where? I'm busy, Igmo. I'm a senior in high school, in case you didn't remember. I can't be driving you around . . .

**Jason**   She says she'd love to! Email me all the info, OK?

**Connor**   It's a deal! Maybe we can hook up and go around together at the convention! I'd really like to meet someone who has the good taste to have the same interest as me.

**Jason**   We will for sure. Later!

**Connor**   *(rising and stretching)* Mom? Oh, Mom? What's for supper?

**Mom**   *(sticking her head in, or re-entering briefly, wiping her hands on a towel)* Hungry? Log on to "www.comehelpmom.com."

**Connor**   Everybody's a "dot comic."

*(CONNOR and MOM exit.)*

**Cassie**   *(as JASON rolls his wheelchair aside to give her access to the computer)* Now what is this you're volunteering me to take you to?

**Jason**   It sounds really great, Cass. See, I've met this guy on-line who's also interested in the war, and there's this convention in his town. He asked me to come meet him so we can hang out together there!

**Cassie**   *(turning her attention away from the computer and back to her brother)* Jace . . . do you think that's such a good idea? To go meet this kid?

**Jason**   I don't think he's a murderer, if that's what you mean. He's my age—you know, he's just a guy! And it's cool to meet somebody else who has the same hobby as me.

        46        

**Cassie**   I don't mean he's a cyber-criminal . . . come on, Jason. Quit pretending you don't know what I'm talking about.

**Jason**   But I don't! *(begins to realize)* Oh wait, Cassie . . . you mean my handicap?

**Cassie**   Don't use that word! You're not handicapped! You just . . .

**Jason**   Can't walk without a wheelchair! Yeah, it's come to my attention.

**Cassie**   All I mean is—if this guy is expecting a friend who can walk all over a convention with him . . .

**Jason**   Then he'll be disappointed, is that what you think? Do you think I should make up an excuse . . . 'gee, sorry, new friend—I have an elephant to wash that day—can't make it'?

**Cassie**   You don't have to get so snotty. I only wondered if you should . . . you know . . . tip him off in advance. Just let him know . . .

**Jason**   That his new Civil War buddy is a wheelchair geek? I don't think so, Cassandra. What if he didn't show up?

**Cassie**   Is that what you think? That he wouldn't show?

**Jason**   I don't know . . . maybe. I just want to go have a good time. If he runs off screaming, I guess I'll just have to deal with it. Now will you take me, if it will fit into your busy schedule? Or do I have to call some "Help the Handicapped" van service to haul my crippled frame to _____ ? *(insert name of city)*

**Cassie**   Oh stop it. Of course I'll take you. Just let me know where and when.

**Jason**    OK. Thanks. *(starts to exits, then stops)* It'll be OK, Cassie. And even if it's not—I'll live, you know?

**Cassie**    Yep. I do.

**Jason**    OK. So hurry up and do your current event, will ya? Do you want to fail and have to stay in high school forever? *(He exits.)*

*(CASSIE types for a moment, then she exits too, looking troubled.)*

*(The next scene takes place at the Civil War Convention. We see banners; perhaps one with "Civil War" marked out to read "The War Between the States." People walk by with Confederate flags, carrying bags which could contain memorabilia, books, etc. Various people are dressed in authentic uniforms of the period, or makeshift uniforms emulating the look of the soldiers. Enter CONNOR and MOM. CONNOR has a fake red rose pinned to his T-shirt.)*

**Connor**    I still think this red rose idea is the worst one I've ever heard. I feel like the biggest fool in the world!

**Mom**    I think it's brilliant. You need some way for . . . what's his name again?

**Connor**    It's Jason, Mom. I've told you twenty times.

**Mom**    OK, so you need some way for Jason to identify you in the middle of all these people. What if you had told him 'I'll be the guy in the jeans and T-shirt.' That would've been really easy. Or—I know—I'll be the guy in the make-pretend Civil War soldier uniform! No one else here had THAT idea!

**Connor**    OK, OK, I get it. No one else for MILES around is wearing a fake red rose. I feel so original!

**Mom**    Some day you'll appreciate my brilliance. *(looking around.)* I wonder if there's a place to get a Coke around here?

# The Same But Different

*(Enter CASSIE pushing JASON in his wheelchair. They stop—JASON looks at his sister for reassurance, then speaks.)*

**Jason**  Hey! Who's the Civil War geek with the red rose pinned to his T-shirt!

*(CONNOR and MOM turn around to the sound of JASON's voice. For a brief moment, they look surprised to see him in his chair. Then CONNOR speaks.)*

**Connor**  Tell her! Tell my mother this rose is the sorriest thing you've ever seen.

**Jason**  It's pretty stupid looking, but I have to say—I had no trouble spotting you. I'm Jason Yeager and this is my sister Cassie.

**Connor**  I'm Connor Sherwood and this is my Mom. Her name is "Mom."

**Mom**  If I'm very good, someday I'll have my own real name! *(shakes hands with JASON and CASSIE)* How nice to meet you. What a great sister to drive your brother to this . . . unique event!

**Cassie**  I'm pretty much the queen of sisters, that's for sure. Nice to meet you, Connor . . . and Connor's Mom. I'm glad to learn there's another boy as weird as my brother. This whole "war" thing is just . . . well . . . not my deal.

**Connor**  Jason, let's get out of here. There's this one guy who has fiber optics representing every battle on this giant map! It's too cool.

**Jason**  I think I saw him on the way in—I definitely want to go spend some time there. Hey, did you see the rifle musket booth? They have three real ones! I mean, authentic!

*Character Education Book of Plays*
*Middle Grade Level*

**Connor**  No! I need a map—I would be really sad if I didn't see a real rifle musket! Where was it?

**Jason**  Back that way.

*(CONNOR moves behind JASON's chair and takes the handles, gently moving CASSIE aside.)*

**Connor**  How do you work this thing?

**Jason**  Let the brake off . . . *(CONNOR lets the brake off with his foot)* and that's all there is to it!

**Connor**  Nice to meet you, Cassie—Mom, I'll see you later. Come on, Jason—let's roll!

**Jason**  So to speak!

**Connor**  I can't help it—just naturally funny. Oh, wait—there's a guy here who's an actual descendant of John Wilkes Booth!

**Jason**  Crazed actors!

**Connor**  No kidding. Did you see . . .

*(They exit, ad libbing about things and people to see. MOM and CASSIE watch them go, then turn to each other.)*

**Mom**  So . . .

**Cassie**  Your son is really nice.

**Mom**  I'm not sure, but I think he may be an alien.

*(a pause, then:)*

**Cassie**  I didn't know if Jason should come . . . you know . . .

# THE SAME BUT DIFFERENT

**Mom**   I think you were perfectly right to bring him, and I think they will be perfectly fine. That chair has nothing to do with the completely weird interest they have in common.

**Cassie**   Yeah . . . that's right, isn't it?

**Mom**   Of course it is—I'm a mother! I'm always right. Now come on, Cassie. Let's go get a Coke—and then I'm just dying to catch the exhibit of Civil War underwear!

**Cassie**   Oh, I'm sorry—did you mean to say . . .

**Mom and Cassie**   The War Between The States!

**Eddie Welch**   *(approaching them)* Actually, ladies—the use of the term "Civil War" is generally accepted by modern scholars. In fact, before the turn of the century . . .

**Cassie**   That underwear exhibit is sounding better all the time!

**Mom**   Let's roll!

*(They escape, laughing, while EDDIE WELCH follows them, saying:)*

**Eddie Welch**   An underwear exhibit? What underwear exhibit? How fascinating! Ladies! Wait for me!

*Character Education Book of Plays*
*Middle Grade Level*

# The Excuse Olympics

## A Play About Responsibility

*Character Education Book of Plays*
*Middle Grade Level*

# The Excuse Olympics

## CAST

**The Sports Commentators**
 Stats Madden
 Sport Gifford

**The Competitors**
 Ben Shirk
 Catrina Noblamo
 Connie Confusion

**The Coaches**
 Ben's Coach
 Catrina's Coach
 Connie's Coach

*Character Education Book of Plays*
*Middle Grade Level*

Copyright ©2001 by Incentive Publications, Inc.
Nashville, TN.

# The Excuse Olympics

## Notes to the Teacher/Director

"Well . . . um . . . I was going to do my homework, but do you know what? I had to . . . um . . . go out of town."

"I did clean up my room, I really did, but my little brother came in and messed it all up again. Really."

"What? I was supposed to empty the dishwasher?! Nobody told me!"

When the students were little, they didn't have much responsibility. They were supposed to eat the little pieces of cereal on their high chair trays and go to sleep when somebody put them down for a nap. But life is different now. Nobody asked their opinion about this, but suddenly they have responsibility everywhere they turn: schoolwork, sports practice, chores, baby-sitting, and play rehearsal!

Maybe it seems like a burden they do not want, but the truth is that it's one of the first steps toward growing up and having the responsibilities they do want.

What about when they do not meet their obligations? Do they face the music, admit that they've messed up, apologize and deal with the consequences, vowing to do better next time—or do they blame somebody else, fabricate obstacles that really were not in their way, or just speak so confusingly that nobody knows what they're talking about?

In *The Excuse Olympics*, each contestant has messed up in some say, and each competes in a mock Olympic setting to give the best excuse. The sportscasters provide commentary on each, and the panel of judges gives them ratings of one to ten. It's a light-hearted look at the lengths to which we will go to avoid not only our responsibilities, but admission of our mistakes.

*Character Education Book of Plays Middle Grade Level*

## Props and Scenery

To put on this play, you will need little in the way of scenery. The sports commentators stand to the side of the stage and the contestants stand center stage. The judges need seats; the panel for the judges can be any table and chairs you have handy. Stats Madden and Sport Gifford, the sportscasters, should wear matching blazers, if you can find them (don't forget about the Salvation Army or Goodwill), and they should have headsets and microphones. Your school probably has a microphone, and you can either borrow a headset or create one out of a coat hanger, with a bit of foam as a mouthpiece.

## Costumes

As for your competitors, you can go one of two ways. Dress them either in regular school clothes, or in sweats or other athletic clothing as if they were really competing in Olympic events. Maybe you can find red, white, and blue t-shirts and shorts or spring for Team USA personalized shirts. Coaches should be dressed in coordinated sweats or t-shirts, and have towels hanging around their necks. Everyone can have those elastic wrist and headbands if you like, also.

Your panel of judges will need a little more in the way of a costume. Principal Peters should wear a suit and tie and maybe some stern looking glasses. Jill Tedley should look just a bit older—remember, she has been jilted (get it? Jill . . . Ted . . . ley?) five times at the altar. She should probably have facial tissue sticking out of all her pockets also, as if she is on the verge of tears at any time. You should be able to have some fun with the mom, Mrs. Veronica Witherspoon. Should she have a diaper bag with diapers sticking out, maybe diaper pins on her shirt—a soccer mom T-shirt or sweatshirt—etc. What does a career mom wear (besides a tired expression)?

# The Excuse Olympics

## Teaching Materials to Accompany *The Excuse Olympics*

1. Improvise a scene between a mom and a son or daughter. Have the mom reprimand the son for forgetting something important, such as studying for a mid-term exam or walking his little sister home from soccer practice. Play the scene two ways. First, have the son make up an excuse, but deliver it as convincingly as possible. (No exaggerating for comic effect—he should try to convince his mom that he's telling the truth.) Have Mom react as she would in that situation. Now—have him tell the truth, apologize, admit to his mistake and promise to be more responsible. How does Mom react now?

2. Play the **Excuse Relay** game. Divide the class or group into two teams. The teacher or group leader presents a charge to the first team, such as "You didn't turn in your homework." Each team member has to come up with a new excuse. "I had to go to the hospital," "I went blind temporarily," "There wasn't a pen in the house," or the old favorite, "My dog ate it." Have a panel of student judges, and one timekeeper—the teams have three minutes to craft as many excuses as possible. The next team gets a different accusation, and so on. Award five points to the team which invents the most excuses within the time limit. Student judges may award extra points for creativity or believability. (Be sure your teacher or group leader has a long list of accusations prepared before you begin to play!)

3. As a class, discuss the responsibilities that class members have at home. How do you feel about them? Do you resent them? Do you feel any pride about the fact that you're able to have responsibility? Do you think having these responsibilities now will do you any good in the future? Explain.

4. Imaginary character Joe is a young man who does not live up to his obligations and responsibilities. He forgets homework, puts his own needs ahead of his family's and friends' and never remembers his chores. Write a paper describing him when he is 30 years old. How will he be? Will he have changed his ways and learned his lesson? Or, is he still shirking responsibility? If you like, write a brief monologue in which you portray this character at your age—and again at age 30.

# The Excuse Olympics

# A Play About Responsibility

*(As the play begins, we see sports commentators STATS MADDEN and SPORT GIFFORD standing together stage right. They have on headsets and are speaking into microphones. A panel of three judges sits stage left, angled so they are visible to the audience. They have stacks of white cards and markers in front of them.)*

**Stats**  Good afternoon, ladies and gentlemen, and welcome to WJHS-TV's *(insert initials of your school)* coverage of this year's Olympic Games! This is Stats Madden, and with me is my co-host—Sport Gifford. Sport?

**Sport**  Stats, it's always a pleasure to experience the exhilaration of the Olympiad. The training that these young people undergo is just incredible, and they're some of the finest competitors the world has ever known.

**Stats**  Well, that's absolutely right, Sport. You don't get to the Olympics by working out only on weekends, that's for sure!

*(They both laugh as though this is something really hilarious.)*

**Sport**  Today's event promises to be one of the more spectacular of this year's Olympic Games. I had the pleasure of watching these young people warm up this afternoon and I was just bowled over!

**Stats**  Yes, Sport, it is exciting to witness these young stars.

*(Competitors begin entering and taking their places center stage. They are bending and stretching, wiping their faces with towels, drinking sports drinks, etc., looking as if they are preparing for some strenuous competition. Each has a coach with him or her, patting them on the backs, rubbing their shoulders, etc.)*

**Stats**  And here they come now, some of the brightest young people ever to represent the United States.

# The Excuse Olympics

**Sport** They'll be competing today in the Excuse-Making event. Would you care to explain a little bit about this tough competition?

**Stats** My pleasure, Sport. Each of these young people had some responsibility in his or her home town—perhaps throwing a paper route, baby-sitting, or simply schoolwork—and for some reason he or she didn't get it done. They will be presenting their most exciting and convincing excuses for the panel of judges today.

**Sport** And just look at that panel of judges! They do look tough, don't they Stats?

**Stats** Well, they're gonna have to be tough to cut through all the stuff that's going to be flying in here later on, if you know what I mean! Let's take a moment to introduce the judges, shall we?

**Sport** You bet. First—here's Principal Peters, principal of Wylie Junior High School *(or insert the name of your school here)*. You gotta believe he's gonna be tough—he's got to have heard it all!

**Stats** Well, that's absolutely right, Sport. Sitting next to Principal Peters is Jill Tedley. Jill's story is a little different—she was engaged to be married no less than five times, but in each case her fiancé backed out!

**Sport** Tragic story, and yet you know she's got to have heard an excuse or two.

**Stats** No doubt about it. Finally—Mrs. Veronica Witherspoon. She's a mother.

**Sport** Enough said! Oh, look—the first competitor seems to be beginning.

# The Excuse Olympics

**Stats**  This is Ben Shirk, from Valrico, Florida. Ben was supposed to take care of his neighbors' house while the family was on vacation, but he didn't go over there once!

**Sport**  Ouch!

**Stats**  Looks like he's getting started—let's listen.

**Ben Shirk**  OK—well, I had every intention of going over to the Picketts' house and taking care of, you know, their lawn and stuff, but some things happened which were completely beyond my control. First, I had the misfortune of running over a nail on my bike which resulted in a flat tire. Thus, I had no way to make it over to their house. However, I made plans to walk the distance, even though it was considerable—but I twisted my ankle on my mother's freshly mopped floor and had to sit with my foot elevated for several days. I tried to enlist the help of my little brother, but he came down with a raging case of chicken pox and was unable to assist me. Undaunted, I procured some crutches and was making plans to limp my way over to the Picketts, when a milkman in a milk delivery truck sideswiped me, causing me to fall down and—believe it or not—sprain my other ankle. I have been cursed with really weak ankles. Still feeling as if I should live up to my responsibility, I tried dragging myself along using my elbows, but a freak thunderstorm roared in, flooding the gutter with torrential rains and reducing my visibility to near zero. I was forced to drag myself back home and, well, I was unable to make it to the Picketts' even once. Thank you.

*(BEN'S COACH puts his arm around BEN and escorts him to the SPORTSCASTERS area. The JUDGES start to write numbers on their cards.)*

**Sport**  Congratulations, Ben, that was an excellent effort!

**Ben Shirk**  Thanks very much. You know, I wasn't sure if I was in the zone today, but I just went out there, got focused, and gave it my best shot.

*Character Education Book of Plays*
*Middle Grade Level*

**Stats**  I was particularly impressed with your use of big words! "Undaunted," "torrential," "misfortune"—that's some pretty serious verbiage! That can't help but increase your believability!

**Ben's Coach**  That was my suggestion to young Ben. I've always felt that if you use big words, good grammar, and sound like you have half a brain, people are going to swallow your unbelievable stories a lot easier. I mean . . . more easily! *(BEN and BEN'S COACH laugh)*

**Sport**  Well, you must be very proud. Ben certainly made a good showing.

**Stats**  You know what else I found impressive? The fact that Ben included weather as part of his excuse. Everyone knows the weather can jump up and bite you in the best laid plans!

**Sport**  Well, that's absolutely right, Stats! Ben's use of a torrential storm in his list of excuses can only help his final score.

**Ben's Coach**  Again, I'm afraid I'll take credit for that. When I competed in the 1980 Winter Olympics, I continually drew on the cold, ice, snow—you name it—and it took me all the way to the gold!

*(The JUDGES begin to lay down their cards and markers.)*

**Sport**  *(as each JUDGE holds up his/her card)* Well, it looks like the judges have their scores—Principal Peters gives Ben—an 8.5! Jill Tedley has written . . . 9.0! And finally Mrs. Veronica Witherspoon comes in low at 7.5. Ouch—that one's going to hurt.

**Stats**  Let's see if we can find out what Mrs. Witherspoon was thinking. *(crossing to MRS. VERONICA WITHERSPOON)* Mrs. Witherspoon? If I might have a quick word?

**Mrs. Veronica Witherspoon**  Very quick, Sonny.

*Character Education Book of Plays*
*Middle Grade Level*

62

# The Excuse Olympics

**Stats**    Why so much lower than your judge pals?

**Mrs. Veronica Witherspoon**    Simple, Sonny. Didn't you hear that kid mention a milkman sideswiping him? That was really a mistake—everyone knows there haven't been milk delivery trucks since there were 15 cent postage stamps! That was completely unbelievable to me, anyway.

**Stats**    You never know what's going to trip these competitors up, do you, ma'am?

**Mrs. Veronica Witherspoon**    Well, that's absolutely right.

*(STATS returns to his position with SPORT)*

**Sport**    That was interesting, Stats! Anyway, Ben, an average score of 8.3333333—not a bad showing at all. Good luck to you, young man!

**Ben**    *(as he and his COACH exit)* Well, I would've done better, but I was so busy thinking of big words to use, and trying to think how to include the weather—plus, I didn't have much time to practice, because of my homework . . .

**Stats**    Making excuses to the bitter end!

**Sport**    What a competitor!

**Stats**    You know, these kids think, live and breathe excuses.

**Sport**    Well that's absolutely right, Stats. *(as CATRINA NOBLAMO and CATRINA'S COACH take center stage.)* And now our second competitor steps up—this is Catrina Noblamo from Des Moines, Iowa. You know, Stats—that name almost sounds like she might be from a South American country!

**Stats**   No chance of that, Sport—she's true red, white, and blue, All American! Her excuse today is an original composition. It seems that Catrina had two reports, a presentation and a science project due for school—and she didn't do either of them!

**Sport**   Whoa! What on earth will she say for her excuse?!

**Stats**   That's an awful lot of responsibility to try and wriggle out of. I hope Catrina's been training hard.

**Sport**   I believe she has, Stats. I think she's tried her excuse out on every teacher at her school—as well as both parents and her grandmother!

**Stats**   Well, let's see how well she's prepared.

**Catrina Noblamo**   OK, look—I know I completely dropped the ball at school this six weeks, but it was just not my fault. Not any of it. See—the day the first report was assigned? I wasn't there—and my friend Cindy took the notes. And when she gave me my notes, she had blotted her lip gloss on them and I couldn't read that part. I could read everything else, but not about the report. OK. Then—when the next report was assigned—like for American History? Well—my teacher speaks in a really low, mumbly tone of voice, like this: *(speaking in a low, mumbly tone of voice)* "Well, boys and girls, I want you to write a report about the pioneers who made their way westward across the prairie . . . " I just couldn't even hear him! And so I was going to go talk to him after class, you know and say like "Dude—what was that assignment?" But when I was headed up toward the desk, this guy behind me stopped me and asked me if he could borrow a pen. So I had to go to my locker and get one—what could I do, be rude to this poor pen-less guy? And then my best friend started talking to me about her boyfriend who broke up with her. And I never got back to American History.

So then—the presentation I had for English class? Well—this was completely not my fault. I was supposed to work on it with, like, three other girls? And we were supposed to meet at Harry's House of Hamburgers and work on it, but there was like no place to work at Harry's without getting ketchup all over our papers, so we just gave up! But is it my fault Harry's House of Hamburgers is, you know, ketchuppy? I don't think so!

And then my science project—well—this is so sad. *(starts to cry)* I started working on growing these little plants with real light and fake light? Like, you know, sunshine and light that would be in the refrigerator? But—the guy at the plant store sold me these plants that were really not healthy—and they died! They just shriveled up and fell over, like this. *(pantomimes plants falling over)* I had really gotten attached to the little green fellas . . . but, you know, that guy sold me sick plants! It was so tragic—but completely not my fault! *(sobs)* Well—that's all I have to say. Thank you.

*(CATRINA'S COACH puts her jacket around her shoulders and gives her a tissue and some water. CATRINA drinks and dabs her eyes as they make their way to the SPORTSCASTERS. The JUDGES write.)*

**Catrina's Coach**  Wasn't she great? What brilliant strategy to blame everybody else for everything she didn't do!

**Sport**  Absolutely inspired, that's all I have to say. Truly a breathtaking effort.

**Catrina**  Thank you so, so much.

**Stats**  The highlight for me has got to be—the crying at the end. That was truly a magnificent touch, Catrina.

**Catrina**  Do you know what's funny? I had never cried at that part before! But today, in the spirit of competition—something just came over me and the tears just flowed. It was an awesome feeling.

**Catrina's Coach**   She is really a natural talent, that's for sure.

**Sport**   There is certainly no denying that. Uh oh—looks like the judges have their scores.

**Stats**   Starting with Principal Peters—he's giving you . . . low marks! 6.5! What is up with that?

**Sport**   Perhaps being in the field of education, he's just sensitive to shirking school responsibility—what do you think, Stats?

**Stats**   That could certainly be it—but look, Jill Tedley gives her—a 10! She gives Catrina a 10! And she seems to be crying herself!

**Catrina**   You know—I was really hoping that she would sympathize with my sadness.

**Sport**   She certainly did sympathize with some part of your competition! A perfect 10 from the judge jilted at the altar. Moving on to Mrs. Veronica Witherspoon—she gives Catrina a low score as well—a 6.0! Even lower than Principal Peters!

**Catrina**   I deserve to win! I do! I had a good presentation and a believable delivery! Those judges just don't know—it's not my fault. They just don't appreciate real talent when they see it!

*(CATRINA'S COACH leads CATRINA off, comforting her, and giving dirty looks to the panel of judges, except for JILL TEDLEY to whom they both blow kisses. They exit.)*

**Stats**   You know, we expected an exciting match today, but I don't think either of us anticipated the kind of raw talent and fierce competition that we're actually witnessing.

**Sport**   Well, that's absolutely right, Stats. And coming front and center now is one of the more impressive competitors of the day, Connie Fusion. Connie was cast in a play and she had a very large role. Well, she didn't learn her lines and what's

*Character Education Book of Plays*
*Middle Grade Level*

66

worse, she missed the final dress rehearsal, letting down the rest of the cast! When the play opened, she was completely unprepared and the whole cast looked bad, all because she had not lived up to her responsibility!

**Stats**  I repeat—ouch! You know, Sport, Connie took the bronze at Sydney *(or insert other Olympic Games site)* and she told me in a recent interview that she feels as if she can take home the gold today if she has perfected her technique.

**Sport**  I don't know about you, Stats, but I think it's entirely possible! Her style is extremely unique. Many have tried to emulate it, but few have come close. Here she is—Connie Fusion.

*(CONNIE'S COACH gives her a quick hug and CONNIE takes center stage, seeming to be breathless, as though she has been hurrying.)*

**Connie**  Oh, I can't believe the traffic, you know what I mean? I mean, I'm just like—whoo! Anyway, I know that you're all thinking, you know, about the play and everything, but you know I just want to say that I didn't, you know—I mean, I just couldn't seem to—OK, let me say it like this. You know how sometimes you just can't seem to get—you know—centered—or you know, your mind just goes—you know, to some place—oh, like if you get distracted from what you're working on—you can relate, can't you? I mean, we all have days—I've just been so, I don't know, not depressed exactly but just like—I can't remember—I just don't seem to know—I mean, I looked at my lines, but then you know, the lights and everything—you can understand what I mean, I know—it was just like—I was just pulling myself in a bunch of directions and I just couldn't! I mean, there was this sale at the mall and then my dogs needed for me to take them to—well, I don't mean me, but like my mom and I had to take them to, you know, the vet—do you know how much responsibility it is to have dogs? I mean, you can relate, can't you? I really liked being in the play—but I just couldn't—you know what I mean? It was just not—you know—I just couldn't settle down and learn. And then my dogs

and the mall got in the way of my . . . you know . . . I mean, I wanted to come to rehearsal, but . . . you know. The end.

*(She bows and CONNIE'S COACH runs up to her and gives her roses. They cross over to SPORT and STATS, as the JUDGES write their scores.)*

**Stats**    Oh my stars and sidelines, that was the most amazing display of confusing speaking I have ever heard! What a brilliant technique!

**Connie's Coach**    *(speaking with a Russian or Romanian-sounding accent.)* We're so proud of Connie. This method of making an excuse is time-honored in my country. The idea is—you start and stop so many times—no one can follow. Do you follow?

**Sport**    Indeed so! I have the feeling that Connie has just completely explained her failure—and yet I have no idea what she just said!

**Stats**    You know, for a second there, I thought she was actually going to finish a sentence!

**Sport**    I know the one you mean—it had the reference to the dogs and the mall in it. I also thought—'oh oh, look out, Connie!' But she pulled it out, chopped it up, and continued to speak confusingly for her entire program.

**Connie**    It's really an effective—you know—like if people think they know what I'm going to say? And then I change? They just nod and smile and wait for me to finish! Oops! That was a whole sentence! You can tell I'm no longer competing!

**Connie's Coach**    Continuous obfuscating can be tiring. It's time to rest now, child.

**Stats**    Scores are being posted—from Principal Peters—a 10! From Jill Tedley—another 10! And finally Mrs. Veronica Witherspoon—also gives Connie Fusion a 10!

**Connie**   Oh, thank you all so much! You know what I mean—I just—it's like—well, you know!

*(As STATS and SPORT speak, the three competitors line up. Each one of the JUDGES puts a medal around each one of the competitors' necks, with the bronze going to CATRINA NOBLAMO, the silver going to BEN SHIRK and the gold going to CONNIE FUSION. Each seems to be filled with emotion.)*

**Sport**   Well, Stats, it's been an emotion-packed afternoon. These young people have obviously worked very hard to perfect the art of making excuses for not living up to their responsibilities.

**Stats**   Makes you wonder, doesn't it, Sport?

**Sport**   What's that, Stats?

**Stats**   As hard as they work to make up excuses—might it just be easier to do what they're supposed to do?

**Sport**   You know, that thought has crossed my mind before. Seems like it's harder to make up these stories, perfect the technique and delivery, and then rehearse how they'll present them.

**Stats**   But then again—with no excuses, we wouldn't have had this fine competition here today, would we Sport?

**Sport**   Well, that's absolutely right, Stats!

**Stats**   This has been Stats Madden . . .

**Sport**   And Sport Gifford for WJHS TV. Join us tomorrow night at nine o'clock eastern time for our live coverage of the Justifying-Crummy-Deeds final competition!

**Stats**   'Til then . . .

**Stats and Sport**   So long!

# But I Want It Now!

## A Mini-Play About Patience

*Character Education Book of Plays*
*Middle Grade Level*

# But I Want It Now!

## CAST

**Stephanie**

**Angela**

# But I Want It Now!

## Notes to the Teacher/Director

Have you ever thought you needed something so badly that you would just DIE if you didn't get it RIGHT THEN!

The truth is, most of us have had this feeling. When we were little, especially—but also as adults, when we need the new house, the new job, the second or third car, the great vacation like all our friends have. We can really get into trouble if we don't have patience.

*But I Want It Now!* is a play about patience. In it, we see one character, Stephanie, at several different stages of her life—when she is ten, thirteen, eighteen, and a mother. In each of the first three scenes, she thinks she must have something NOW; these three things are: a bike, to be allowed to go to a concert, and to go out with her boyfriend. As she writes in her diary at the end of each scene; we see the benefits that result from Stephanie's patience. In the final scene, Stephanie is joined by her daughter, Angela, as Angela wrestles with some patience issues of her own.

This play is almost a monologue. The actress playing Stephanie will have the challenge of portraying the character at these different stages of her life. There are several ways to create this illusion. Her voice can start out higher and then gradually become more mature. Since she remains on stage until the scene where she is the mom, only minimal costume changes can happen—maybe her hair can start out in a pony tail, then be taken down, then pulled into a baseball cap.

During the time passing portions of the play, it would be ideal if you could dim the lights. Playing pre-recorded music would work well also—maybe something youthful for the scene in which Stephanie is ten, some popular teen music for the thirteen-year-old Stephanie and a love ballad for the older girl. Perhaps the same song could be played before the Angela scene.

Stephanie's bedroom needs to be created on stage. Best—an actual bed with bedspread, stuffed animals and pillows. Good—chairs or desks pushed together and covered with a bedspread, stuffed animals and pillows. If at all possible, do hang posters and pictures of the different periods of her life on the walls or flats of your performance area—this will help prevent audience confusion.

*Character Education Book of Plays*
*Middle Grade Level*

# But I Want It Now!

## Teaching Materials to Accompany *But I Want It Now!*

1. As a class, discuss the kinds of trouble adults can get into if they don't exercise patience, especially in terms of finances and credit.

2. So what if our parents give us everything we want, when we want it? What's wrong with that? Write a brief paper discussing how a person might turn out who is given everything he or she wants for his or her whole young life.

3. Try your hand at writing monologues related to this mini-play. You might write a monologue as though you were Amanda the night of the concert, discussing how it felt to be taken downtown by the police and have your parents come pick you up. You might be Stephanie's mom, wrestling with her feelings of wanting to please her daughter, but wanting to teach her about patience, too. Or, if you can hand in your work privately, maybe you are Travis, expressing your feelings after breaking up with Stephanie. Are there other characters whose thoughts and feelings could be explored by a one-person scene? You decide.

4. If you do not have one already, start a diary. Nothing is more interesting than re-reading about earlier times of your life. Do not feel as if you have to write every day; it's not a homework assignment. Just record your ideas as your life unfolds, write the things that you don't care to discuss out loud with anyone. Your diary will be a treasure for later days in your life.

# But I Want It Now!

# A Mini-Play About Patience

*(The mini-play takes place in STEPHANIE's bedroom. We see her bed with many stuffed animals on it. If it is possible, there should be youthful, feminine posters and pictures on the wall—ponies, kitties, the latest cartoon fad. STEPHANIE, age 10, enters, obviously furious, and throws herself onto her bed.)*

**Stephanie**   It's not fair, it's just not fair! All I want is a new bike! That's all! But what does my mother say? 'No, Stephanie, not now, we can't afford it. Maybe you'll get one for your birthday.' But my birthday isn't for *(counts on her fingers)* TEN MORE MONTHS! How can I possibly wait that long? By the time I turn eleven, I probably won't even WANT to ride bikes anymore! I probably won't even be friends with Amanda and Megan—they have new bicycles and they get to ride all around the neighborhood and what do I have? *(getting off bed and beginning to stomp around)* My brother's hand-me-down! With a bar across the middle! It's too embarrassing! I want a new bike and I want it NOW! Oh, why do I have to have the parents I have? They say I should be patient! They say 'Good things come to those who wait'! Well, I won't wait, I won't! I want it NOW!

*(She throws herself onto her bed and collapses into sobs. The lights dim, or music plays—passage of time is indicated. A stage hand wheels in a great looking bike. STEPHANIE sits up, still the same age, and begins to write in her diary, reading her entry as she writes.)*

Dear Diary—Happy eleventh birthday to me! It was the best birthday ever. Megan, Amanda, and all my friends came over. We played games and had cake and ice cream sundaes that we decorated ourselves! And guess what? Mom and Dad got me the greatest bike I've ever seen! It's purple with spots on it—

*Character Education Book of Plays
Middle Grade Level*

with a basket and a horn and a place to hang a water bottle. *(or describe the bicycle used in the scene)* It's the coolest. I feel rotten that I've thrown such fits, not wanting to wait for my bike. Mom says they could never have afforded this one when I started asking for one. I hereby promise never to be so—bratty and impatient ever again! Well, goodnight—I'm eleven!

*(STEPHANIE sleeps. Stage hands remove stuffed animals, perhaps leaving one, and all little girl posters. They replace them with a few CD cases on her bed and posters of boy bands and current teen stars. When they finish, STEPHANIE wakes up and stretches.)*

Ahh—Saturday—no school! Nobody ever told me seventh grade was going to be this hard. But at least it's . . . *(sitting up in bed, angrily realizing something)* it's Saturday, the day of the Dead Men Walking concert which my parents will not let me go to! *(getting out of bed and stomping around her room)* How could I forget?! I am the only one of my group who isn't allowed to go—*(mocking her parents)* 'We don't think it's a good environment for you, Stephanie. There will probably be drugs! And the lyrics of those songs aren't suitable.' My life isn't suitable! Megan and Amanda are going, and Brian and Jared . . . *(sarcastically)* and I guess their lives will be ruined! Their little minds are going to be polluted forever by lyrics of Dead Men Walking songs! And they'll become drug addicts tonight because some people around them are doing drugs! I am thirteen years old and my parents treat me like I'm a baby in diapers! *(mocking her parents again)* 'Maybe when you're older, Stephanie. But no heavy metal concerts now.' But I WANT to go NOW! I probably won't even like this kind of music when I'm old enough to go! That's probably what they're counting on . . . oh, I hate my life.

*(She throws herself back into her bed. Time passes, indicated by lights or music. She begins writing in her diary.)*

Dear Diary—hi, it's me, feeling very stupid. Remember the Dead Men Walking concert? Well—it turns out they were selling alcohol to minors, and the police raided it. A whole lot

# But I Want It Now!

of kids got taken downtown, including Amanda—Megan hid behind somebody's car and they didn't see her. Anyway, everybody's parents had to come down and take them home—a bunch of kids were throwing up because they'd had too much to drink and it was just gross. You may remember that I didn't get to go—I was at home watching a rented video with my parents and my brother. Amanda's mother called my mother and they talked about it—that's how I found out. My mother told me what happened, but you know what was weird? She never said anything like 'See? I told you you shouldn't go' or anything like that. She just said 'I'm glad you are home, safe and sound.' and we went back to watching our movie. I really don't want to think that my parents know anything . . . I really want to think that I should be able to do whatever I want whenever I want . . . but this sure was lucky. Oh well—good night. I hope Megan and Amanda are OK.

*(STEPHANIE goes to sleep again. Now stage hands remove previous room decorations, except possibly the same special stuffed animal, and put up college pennants, homecoming corsages and other keepsakes. When they finish, STEPHANIE, now age 18, gets up and begins to pace.)*

What in the world do I do? I like Travis so much—we've been going together since the first week of junior year—I guess I love him, really. I mean, I feel safe with him, and he's so much fun to be around. But he's wanting things to move faster than I think they should. I don't dare talk to my parents—I know what they would say—'You need to wait, Stephanie. If he's really the one, he'll have patience.' And I know they would be right—but it's not just him—it's me too. I need a big dose of patience right now because part of me feels like I better take this step or he's gone, you know? And I don't want to lose him. What in the world do I do? The senior prom is this weekend and everybody in our crowd is staying out all night, but my parents say I have to be home by 3:00 a.m. I know I should be mad at them for giving me a curfew, but in a way it might make things easier. Oh what in the world do I do?

# But I Want It Now!

*(Time passes. STEPHANIE is very happy. She is writing in her diary.)*

Dear Diary—I can't believe I've almost filled up another diary! I'm so happy to write two things: First and best, I have a full scholarship to University of Texas at Austin *(or insert favorite college)*. I can't wait to start getting my stuff together for my dorm. I wonder who my roommate will be. And here's the other thing. Remember Travis? Well, when I told him how I felt, he completely broke up with me. He called me names and said I'd been leading him on . . . what a creep. I was sad, of course, but what if . . . what if? I'll just leave it at that. I bet there's somebody wonderful waiting for me at U.T.— somebody who will think like me and likes the music I like . . . and NOT Dead Men Walking! Yuck! Can you believe I ever liked that guy!? Anyway, I look forward to meeting someone—but I'm not going to rush into anything. I'll be patient.

*(This time STEPHANIE exits. The room is restored to the little girl's room, but with different posters and pictures. The same stuffed animal that was in all three scenes is on this bed, however, with some new ones. Enter ANGELA, age 10, stomping around and acting as if she is really furious.)*

**Angela**    Ohhh, my parents make me so mad! Both of them! All I want is a jet-powered skateboard—that's all! All of my friends have one—but not me! No, I have to wait until Christmas! That's forever! *(throws herself on the bed)* I think I'll run away from home. I think I'll starve myself as a protest. I think I'll . . .

*(We hear a knock on the door and STEPHANIE enters. Now she is the mom. She sits next to ANGELA and puts her arm around her daughter.)*

**Stephanie**    Angela, honey, come back downstairs. Your dad and I want to have a little visit with you about patience. You may not believe this—but I know exactly how you feel.

# But I Want It Now!

**Angela** You? How could you know how I feel? You have everything you ever wanted! This house that you love, my dad who is a lawyer and you think is so great . . .

**Stephanie** And you and your brother.

**Angela** Who's gross . . .

**Stephanie** Who are great, both of you . . .

**Angela** You've gotten everything you ever wanted your whole life! I bet you just said to Grandma, 'Mom! Get me a . . . something . . . ' and she just hopped right off to the store.

**Stephanie** Yes, that's pretty much how it was. Oh, silly, come on downstairs and we'll talk about this.

*(ANGELA stalls, smoothing the covers on her bed, getting a stuffed animal, etc.)*

**Stephanie** Angela? Some time today?

**Angela** Mom, please—I'm coming, I'm coming! Could you have a little patience?

**Stephanie** Patience? Me? Why Angela—let me tell you a couple of stories . . .

*(STEPHANIE smiles and exits with her daughter.)*

*Character Education Book of Plays*
*Middle Grade Level*

# Captain Commitment

## A Play About Commitment

*Character Education Book of Plays*
*Middle Grade Level*

# Captain Commitment

## CAST

**Captain Commitment / Mark Trent** *(his secret identity)*

**Lewis Lane,** *reporter for* **The Daily Comet**

**Kimmy Olsen.** *reporter and photographer for* **The Daily Comet**

**Larry Black,** *editor for* **The Daily Comet**

**Football Player #1**

**Football Player #2**

**Cheerleader #1**

**Cheerleader #2**

**Band Member #1**

**Drill Team Girl #1**

# Captain Commitment

## Notes to the Teacher/Director

In generations past, it really meant something profound to give your word. If a person said he would do something, then he absolutely would, barring unforeseen illness or accident. He had given his word.

In today's world, some people are losing sight of the idea of making a commitment and following through. We say we'll do something, and we mean it . . . unless something more fun comes along, or unless it becomes in some way inconvenient or unpleasant to do the thing we said we would do—then we start making up excuses or leaving messages on people's answering machines saying we won't help them move, come to work, run an errand, etc. One woman was asked why she didn't feel guilty when she backed out of commitments she had made. Her answer? "I guess I just changed my mind." We should not "change our minds," once we have given our word.

It is not only about commitment to others. Many people are more likely to hire people with college degrees not only because of the knowledge they have gained by working the courses, but because it is evident that the person with the degree set a goal for himself or herself—made a commitment to follow through—and did what was needed to achieve that goal and keep that commitment.

*Captain Commitment* is a silly, light-hearted play that deals with this idea. "CC" is on the planet trying very hard to convince people to live up to their commitments. He must start with Lewis Lane and Kimmy Olsen, his co-workers at The Daily Comet. (Captain Commitment's secret identity, Mark Trent, works there as a reporter.) He then progresses to Eastwood High School, where half of the football team has decided not to play the big game. They're just tired of losing and tired of working out; they want to go to the movies instead. After a pep rally from Captain Commitment, they decide to live up to their commitments—to family, coaches, teachers, and friends—and play after all. Mark Trent has the scoop for *The Daily Comet*.

# Captain Commitment

## Props and Scenery

You will need a couple of stools or chairs for Captain Commitment at the beginning of the play, and a desk for the reporters at the newspaper. A few props will be needed: a can of soda or candy bar for Captain Commitment, reporter props for Kimmy and Lewis, a camera on a strap, notebooks and pens, and whatever else would clutter up a reporter's desk. The high school students need a few things to establish their characters: a football helmet or two, a football, pompons, athletic bags, etc.

## Costumes

As for costumes, the biggest challenge will be, of course, Captain Commitment's superhero costume. You can go as far as you like (bearing in mind that he has to jump in and out of Mark Trent's clothes pretty rapidly.) He should, of course, have a t-shirt or long-sleeved top with a big CC on the front. A cape could be fashioned out of any fabric and tied in a knot at his neck. (If you end up with a really silly and cumbersome cape that is in no way hidden by his secret identity clothes, you could add a line for Kimmy at the end of the play such as "Do you think we're blind? You think we can't see that silly bath towel tied at your neck?") Tights might be a bit far to go—or maybe he wears walking shorts with tights underneath. If he does not wear tights, you can replace the line "I do look pretty good in a pair of tights" with "I bet I would look good in a pair of tights."

As for his secret identity clothing, choose whatever would fit over his superhero costume quickly—probably a jacket and a pair of slacks. Kimmy Olsen, Lewis Lane, and Larry Black can wear either regular business clothing, or stylized press clothes from earlier days, such as a hat with a sign saying PRESS sticking out of the band, and tailored business suits. The costumes for the high school kids should be pretty obvious, and easy to round up. Since they do not have to change into or out of the costumes, it might be fun to use authentic costumes, with full cheerleader, football team, band, and drill team uniforms.

# Captain Commitment

## Teaching Materials to Accompany *Captain Commitment*

1. Write a brief paper describing how your life would be if every adult decided to skip his or her commitments. Of course think of your parents and teachers, but do not stop there—how about the guy who runs the gas station? The grocery store? Your favorite stores in the mall?

2. As a class, discuss times when someone has made a commitment to you, then let you down. How did you feel? Have you ever backed out of a commitment to someone, only to feel rotten about it later?

3. Hold a contest to see who can design the best costume for Captain Commitment. Have the class vote. The winning designer gets to appoint a committee to help him or her create the costume.

4. This play is obviously "spoofing" or poking gentle fun at the *Superman* television shows, movies and comic books. What if it had been based on *Batman* or *Spiderman* instead? Try your hand at re-writing one of the scenes in that fashion.

# Captain Commitment

## A Play About Commitment

*(As the play begins, we see CAPTAIN COMMITMENT sitting center stage on a stool or chair. He is drinking a soft drink or eating a candy bar, and looks downcast. He is dressed in his superhero costume, and a jacket and pair of pants are on another chair nearby. He takes one last drink or bite, then addresses the audience.)*

**Captain Commitment**  Hey everybody—Captain Commitment here. What's up? *(he sighs and puts down his soda or crumples his candy paper)* I guess you can tell by looking at my outfit that I'm a superhero. Which is not an easy job, let me tell you. Especially lately. I'll explain. On my home planet, if we say we're going to do something, we do it. End of story. No excuses, no wriggling out of it—we follow through. *(stands and begins to walk back and forth in front of the audience)* But then I get here, to Earth—and it's a whole different story.

*(Enter newspaper reporters LEWIS LANE and KIMMY OLSEN. Either pre-set a desk for them, or have them bring on their desk. KIMMY is a photographer, and she has a camera around her neck on a strap. LEWIS has a notebook and pencil. They are oblivious to CAPTAIN COMMITMENT and compare notes in LEWIS's notebook.)*

In my secret identity as Mark Trent I work here at this newspaper. It's called the Daily Comet. I guess the name appealed to me—Comet . . . Commit . . . get it? Anyway, these characters behind me are Lewis Lane and Kimmy Olsen.

**Larry Black**  *(from offstage)* Lewis? Kimmy? Mark? Why isn't that story on my desk?

# Captain Commitment

| | |
|---|---|
| **Captain Commitment** | That's our editor and boss, Larry Black. I guess I'd better suit up and get to work. *(he starts to put on his secret identity outfit, the clothes which were on the other chair)* Now—just watch how this goes. It's enough to make a superhero's scalp itch! |

*(CAPTAIN COMMITMENT finishes dressing as MARK TRENT and enters the scene.)*

| | |
|---|---|
| **Lewis Lane** | There you are, Mark! I was wondering if you were gone for the day. |
| **Kimmy Olsen** | Gee, Mr. Trent—I'm really glad you're not! |
| **Lewis Lane** | That's right. We need your help on this story! |
| **Mark Trent** | What's the assignment, guys? |
| **Larry Black** | *(entering, shaking his fist and blustering)* I'll tell you what the assignment is! It's to finish this story before six o'clock tonight! These two slackers are doing crossword puzzles or something out here—I haven't seen one word about the situation at Eastwood High School! |
| **Lewis Lane** | Aw, Chief—that's not fair. We've been on the phones all afternoon, calling kids, talking to parents . . . |
| **Kimmy Olsen** | I went out there and got some great shots . . . of kids leaving school, or sitting around, doing nothing . . . |
| **Mark Trent** | What's going on at the high school? |
| **Larry Black** | Well, Mark—since at least YOU seem to care . . . I'll bring you up to speed. It seems that there was a big football game scheduled tonight, between Eastwood High School and its cross-town rival . . . |
| **Mark Trent** | Don't tell me—Westwood High School. |

# Captain Commitment

**Larry Black**   No, actually the name of the school is Newman High School. You know, Paul Newman? Clint Eastwood? Get with the program, Trent!

**Mark Trent**   Sorry, Mr. Black.

**Lewis Lane**   So what happens is—bunches of the kids just decided that they didn't want to bother to show up for the game! Half the football team decided they'd rather watch some TV or go get a burger . . .

**Kimmy Olsen**   Then several of the cheerleaders decided they would bail too, and they all went to the mall . . .

**Larry Black**   The drill team is at the stadium, walking around not knowing what to do . . .

**Kimmy Olsen**   They already had their shiny hose on!

**Lewis Lane**   Only the band continued practicing and marching on the completely empty field.

**Larry Black**   No one knows what's come over these kids! Are they sick with a lazy disease? Have they lost their minds because of too much Algebra? Have their bodies been inhabited by aliens who don't know the importance of high school sports? We need to find out!

**Mark Trent**   Right, Chief—we'll get on it right away.

**Larry Black**   See that you do! I want that story on my desk by six o'clock or you're all three out of a job. *(starts to exit)* And don't call me Chief! *(he storms out)*

**Mark Trent**   What do you think, guys? Should we go out to the high school and talk to these kids? Find out what's going on?

**Lewis Lane**   We probably should . . .

*Character Education Book of Plays*
*Middle Grade Level*

# Captain Commitment

| | |
|---|---|
| **Kimmy Olsen** | It is such a weird story . . . |
| **Lewis Lane** | I would like to know why these kids are acting so bizarre . . . |
| **Kimmy Olsen** | But I have a conflict. My little sister is getting married and there's a shower for her tonight! |
| **Lewis Lane** | I really wanted to get the oil changed in my car before the weekend. |
| **Mark Trent** | But Mr. Black wants the story by six! Are you two going to work on it or not? |
| **Kimmy Olsen** | I know we really should . . . |
| **Lewis Lane** | I sure do need to get my car looked at, though . . . |
| **Mark Trent** | Will you two excuse me for a minute? I have something I need to check on in the janitor's closet down the hall. |
| **Kimmy Olsen** | Sure, Mark. |
| **Lewis Lane** | We may not be here when you get back, though . . . |
| **Mark Trent** | Oh, I bet you will. See ya! |

*(As MARK TRENT takes off his secret identity clothes to reveal his CAPTAIN COMMITMENT costume, he talks to the audience.)*

| | |
|---|---|
| **Captain Commitment** | Do you see what I mean? Kimmy and Lewis work here at the paper, this is their job, but they're about to try to sneak out of their commitment to finish this story. Well—we'll soon see about that. *(he "flies" back into the scene)* |
| **Lewis Lane** | *(looking up from his desk where he has been gathering up papers and preparing to leave)* Captain Commitment! |
| **Kimmy Olsen** | He's so dreamy! |

# Captain Commitment

| | |
|---|---|
| **Captain Commitment** | Lewis . . . Kimmy . . . I think we need to have a little talk. |
| **Lewis Lane** | About what, Captain Commitment? |
| **Kimmy Olsen** | We can talk about anything you like, "CC." |
| **Captain Commitment** | We need to have a word about . . . commitment. |
| **Kimmy Olsen** | Commitment? |
| **Lewis Lane** | What an odd thing for Captain Commitment to talk to us about! |
| **Captain Commitment** | You have a story due at six o'clock, don't you? |
| **Lewis Lane** | Well . . . yes . . . but we've got other stuff we need to take care of! |
| **Kimmy Olsen** | My sister's bridal shower! *(flirting with CAPTAIN COMMITMENT)* Gee—I wish somebody would throw me a bridal shower . . . |
| **Lewis Lane** | And my car's oil needs changing! We can't devote our lives to this paper! |
| **Captain Commitment** | No one is asking you to do that, Lewis. But you do work here . . . and Larry Black did ask for that story by six—you have a commitment to him to deliver! Not to mention your commitment to this newspaper and to all your readers who want to know what's going on! |
| **Kimmy Olsen** | You know, Lewis—he's right. Mr. Black is counting on us! |
| **Lewis Lane** | I guess you do have a point, Captain Commitment. I started working for a newspaper because I wanted to keep people informed . . . *(he faces the audience, and looks off into the distance as though he is remembering something very dramatic)* To let the people of the community know what is |

*Character Education Book of Plays*
*Middle Grade Level*

# Captain Commitment

happening, to give them the information they need from day to day. *(facing the others again, "back to reality")* Plus, I really needed the paycheck.

**Captain Commitment**   So I can count on you to get the story written by six?

**Kimmy Olsen**   You bet, Captain Commitment! And I'll go develop these super pictures to go with it!

**Lewis Lane**   And I'll go grab a computer and start writing what I know so far. Thanks, Captain Commitment!

*(KIMMY OLSEN and LEWIS LANE exit, striking their props and desk. CAPTAIN COMMITMENT addresses the audience again.)*

**Captain Commitment**   OK, that went pretty well. Kimmy and Lewis are good kids; they just need a little reminding now and then. But do you see what I mean? Just let something be the slightest bit inconvenient, and people are ready to bail. Well—I guess I'd better get over to the high school and find out what this is all about. *(as he "flies" he says the following in the spirit of "Up, up and away!" a phrase commonly said by . . . another superhero:)* Meet your commitments today!

*(Now we are at Eastwood High School. There are several band members holding instruments and playing or talking; two or three football players standing together looking worried, several drill team girls stretching, and two cheerleaders walking by carrying bags and pompons. CAPTAIN COMMITMENT "flies" into their midst.)*

**Football Player #1**   Hey, look everybody! It's Captain Commitment!

*(Everyone starts to gather around CAPTAIN COMMITMENT.)*

**Cheerleader #1**   I am so not believing that Captain Commitment is here at our school! This is like so outrageous!

**Cheerleader #2**   He looks a little shorter than I thought he would.

**Captain Commitment**   I heard that!

# Captain Commitment

**Cheerleader #2**   Sorry . . .

**Band Member #1**   Why are you here, Captain Commitment? Are you chasing a criminal?

**Captain Commitment**   No, young people, I'm here to talk to you.

**Drill Team Girl #1**   To us? What did we do?

**Captain Commitment**   It's what you didn't do, young lady.

**Football Player #1**   What do you mean?

**Captain Commitment**   What's this I hear about everyone bailing on the game tonight?

**Cheerleader #1**   Oh, that! I thought it was something important.

**Football Player #2**   We've just had it, Captain Commitment! We've worked hard all season—in the heat when school first started—

**Football Player #1**   And for what? We always lose . . . we're tired . . . we just want to blow it all off and watch a little TV.

**Football Player #2**   Or take our girlfriends to the movies.

**Cheerleader #1**   And us cheerleaders? Well, we don't care—we're here to cheer for our guys if they're playing—but if they're not, hey—we're outta here.

**Cheerleader #2**   There's a sale on Tommy jeans at Foley's! *(or insert trendy clothing item and store here)*

**Cheerleader #1**   Oh, come on! Tommy is so last spring!

**Captain Commitment**   So, let me get this straight. Nobody is ill . . .

**All**   *(ad libbing agreeing responses)* No, no, nobody's sick . . .

# Captain Commitment

**Captain Commitment**   And you're supposed to play tonight, but you just think you'll skip out and go have some fun?

**Football Player #1**   Yep—that's pretty much it, wouldn't you say, guys?

**All**   *(again ad libbing agreeing responses)* Yes, that's right.

**Captain Commitment**   Well, I have a message from your parents. They're all going to quit their jobs and lie around watching soap operas all day munching on snacks. That is, until the money for snacks runs out.

**Football Player #2**   What are you talking about, Captain Commitment? Our parents didn't really call you, did they?

**Captain Commitment**   No, young people, I'm just making a point. Your parents have a commitment to take care of you. They go to work to make money to pay for your house, your food, your clothing. They just don't decide they've had it one day and head for the beach!

**Cheerleader #2**   That actually happened once in our house! My mother just started yelling about how she'd had it with my brothers and sisters and me and she drove off! We finally found her drinking iced tea in a lounge chair on the beach. It was too funny! She came home, though, and made dinner.

**Captain Commitment**   Why do you think she came home?

**Cheerleader #2**   She had gotten enough sun?

**Captain Commitment**   Maybe, but I doubt it. I bet it was because she had commitments to attend to back at the house. Like cooking dinner for you kids, even though you were making her nuts. This is my point: you guys have tried out for these teams and squads, and you've made it. Your teachers and sponsors have worked with you, coached you, taught you routines and

# Captain Commitment

cheers. When you signed up for football, or the drill team, or the band . . .

**Band Member #1**  Hey! The band showed up!

**Captain Commitment**  That's right, I forgot. Everybody but the band is failing to live up to their commitment. The rest of the team is counting on you—the parents are looking forward to seeing a game and cheering along with you cheerleaders. You have a commitment here—and just because it's become boring or tiring doesn't mean it doesn't exist.

**Football Player #1**  But we lose, lose, LOSE! Every week! It's discouraging! No wonder we want to go to the movies.

**Captain Commitment**  Well, now's not the time to quit! Re-commit yourself to the team, to extra practice, or whatever it takes to beat Newman High School.

**Cheerleader #1**  You know, Captain Commitment, you could really be a cheerleader yourself!

**Captain Commitment**  I do look pretty good in a pair of tights.

**Cheerleader #2**  What do you say, guys? One more time for old Eastwood High?

**Football Player #2**  Yeah, I guess Captain Commitment is right. We do have an obligation to mop up the field with those creeps from Newman! I'll go find the rest of the guys—we'll be on the field in fifteen minutes!

**Football Player #1**  Many apologies, everybody—I guess we were just feeling a little sorry for ourselves.

**Captain Commitment**  Everybody does, now and then! Now get ready to go, fight, win! And band members—way to go!

# Captain Commitment

*(CAPTAIN COMMITMENT and all the high school kids exit excitedly, ready to do their part in tonight's game. KIMMY OLSEN and LEWIS LANE re-enter, carrying sheets of paper and photographs.)*

**Lewis Lane**    What a great scoop! This really came together! "High School On Strike—Players Walk Out!" Let's see those pictures.

**Kimmy Olsen**    Here's a great one. See—the guys are walking away from the field house, looking down? It's so dramatic, don't you think?

**Lewis Lane**    It's dramatic for sure. Oh, and I like this one—two cheerleaders running smack into each other!

**Kimmy Olsen**    I think they were headed for two different malls. This is going to be a great story!

*(CAPTAIN COMMITMENT, now in his MARK TRENT clothes, re-enters.)*

**Mark Trent**    Hold on, you two! I have late-breaking news on the story at Eastwood!

**Lewis Lane**    What?! We're all finished!

**Mark Trent**    But I've just come from the high school, and the game's back on! See, Captain Commitment showed up there and gave a little pep rally about their commitments to their families, coaches, teachers and each other! They came to their senses and re-committed to playing tonight! I'll just head for a computer, and type up the revised story!

**Lewis Lane**    Hold on a minute, Mark. How do you know Captain Commitment showed up at the high school? I thought you were in the janitor's closet!

**Mark Trent**    Why, er . . . I passed Captain Commitment on his way over there and I tagged along.

# Captain Commitment

**Kimmy Olsen**   Oh, come on, Mark, quit playing around. Everybody here at the paper knows you're really Captain Commitment, in his secret identity!

**Mark Trent**   What?!

**Lewis Lane**   That's right, Mark, we were just having a little fun with you. We've known for years! I mean, look at yourself! You don't look one bit different! You don't even have a fake mustache or a pair of corny glasses!

**Kimmy Olsen**   What do you think, we're blind?

**Mark Trent**   I . . . I don't know what to say!

**Lewis Lane**   Well, you can start by saying thank you. We decided a long time ago to keep your secret. I mean, it would've been a great scoop for the *Daily Comet* to expose Captain Commitment's secret identity . . . but then you would stop doing your thing. And that wouldn't have helped anybody!

**Mark Trent**   Gee—thanks, guys.

**Kimmy Olsen**   Don't mention it. Just think of it as our commitment to you! Now, let's get started on that story—we still have a deadline!

*(They all put their arms around each others' shoulders and laugh, then freeze. MARK TRENT sneaks out, leaving the other two frozen.)*

**Mark Trent**   OK, so I'm busted here. I guess a man can't keep making trips to the janitor's closet forever. Anyway, remember, everybody—if you keep commitments you make to others, you're really keeping the most important commitment of all—to yourself. So—

*(KIMMY OLSEN and LEWIS LANE unfreeze and join "MARK TRENT," saying:)*

Meet your commitments today!

# Yeah, Me Too!

## A Monologue About Loyalty

# One Frog's Story

## A Monologue About Courage

## Notes to the Teacher/Director

Here are two monologues which can be performed individually or together. As they are written, *Yeah, Me Too!* is a monologue for a girl, and *One Frog's Story* is for a boy.

*Yeah, Me Too!* deals with loyalty. Alissa works very hard to go along with her crowd and never rock the boat. They want to bowl, she wants to bowl—they want to catch a movie, so does she—and when they say they do not like her best friend Laura, she agrees, saying she does not like her either sometimes. Where is her loyalty to her long-time best friend? Religion plays an important role in Alissa's life, but she quickly denies her enjoyment of church when her friends say they don't like it and think it's dumb. Where is her loyalty to her faith? And finally, when the talk turns to creepy parents and how awful they can be, Alissa is right in there too, even though she actually likes her parents very much and has to make up some complaints. Again—a serious shortage of loyalty to family. Now Alissa is confused about why her friends do not seem to want to spend as much time with her as they once did. Any ideas?

*One Frog's Story* is about drugs and alcohol and how we can trick ourselves into thinking they're going to change us into something better. Our hero, Frog, gets invited to take some magic stuff which will turn him into whatever he wants to be—a cooler, better-looking frog, a fierce owl, or even a human being. He is hesitant, feeling that it may not be good for him, but he doesn't have the nerve

to stand up to his friends who are all excited about this chance to turn into something great. So they drink the potion and take the pills, but guess what—he and his pals feel rotten after they have taken several doses, and are still absolutely the same frogs they were before. He feels dumb.

## Scenery and Costumes

The characters in the first monologue can wear normal school clothes, and the Frog can wear solid green, or green and brown. You may wish to experiment with theatrical make-up, looking at a cartoon picture of a frog to get an idea of how to apply the make-up. No scenery is needed, unless you would like for one of the actors to be able to sit on a stool.

## Teaching Materials to Accompany *Yeah, Me Too!*, and *One Frog's Story*

1. As a class, discuss why Alissa's friends are probably not very excited about hanging around with her too much anymore. After all, she's going along with everything they suggest—why would this not inspire loyalty in them?

2. Write a brief paper describing a time in which you were not completely loyal to someone or something for the sake of going along with someone else, perhaps someone you were anxious to impress. Think in terms of your friends, your school, your family members. If you can't recall such an experience, discuss how Alissa's behavior demonstrates a lack of loyalty to herself.

3. Write a monologue in the character of Laura. Did someone tell her what Alissa said about her? Did she overhear it? Did Alissa behave in a disloyal fashion in front of Laura? How does Laura feel?

4. Write a rap song or poem as though you are Frog. You may wish to choose an existing song and re-write the lyrics to it, or make up a rhythm and rhyme of your own.

5. Discuss the idea of self-acceptance with regard to attempting to be somebody else through drugs or alcohol. Does this ever work? What are some positive ways of improving the way we feel about ourselves?

# A Monologue About
## Loyalty

**Alissa**   Hi, my name is Alissa, and I'm really confused about something. Maybe if I talk about it I can figure it out. *(takes a deep breath)* Here goes.

I used to have a lot of really great friends. My best friend, Laura, lives next door to me. We met when we were little, and we have been best friends ever since. I met the rest of my gang at school—like five girls who were really close to me, and even three guys, if you can imagine. They would come over on the weekends sometimes, and we'd hang out, or my mother would take us to a movie, stuff like that. I always went along with whatever anybody else wanted to do. Like if someone would say, "I'd like to go to a movie!" I'd say "Me, too." I never "rocked the boat," as my mother would say.

Sometimes it was tricky to just go along and never make waves. Like one time, Laura wanted to go with me and my other friends. One of the girls in my group said she didn't really like Laura and didn't want her to go. So I said, "Yeah, I know what you mean. Laura does some things that really

102

make me crazy." I didn't mean it—Laura doesn't do anything to make me crazy, she's my best friend! But I didn't want to make the other girl mad, you know? I wanted to get along.

Maybe somebody told Laura I said that—I haven't seen her in about two weeks.

Also, my family goes to church every week, and we always have. I really like going; it gives me a good feeling. Well, some of the guys in my group started saying they didn't like going to church, that it was dumb. I told them that my parents made me go and I thought it was dumb, too. I can't believe I said that! I love going to church. I just wanted to agree with the guys.

Here's something else that made me feel crummy. I have really great parents. They're nice and funny and, as long as I do what I'm supposed to do, they are never mean to me. Well, one day my friends and I were walking home from school, and some of the kids started griping about their parents, about how they were all strict and stuff, and made the kids do chores and never let them have any fun. Can you believe it—I joined right in! I picked a few things to gripe about that were a little bit true, and then I just made some stuff up! If my mom or dad had somehow walked up behind me on the sidewalk, I would've died! But everybody was talking bad about their parents, so I thought I'd better do the same—I didn't want to be the only geek who likes her mom and dad!

Lately, my friends haven't been calling as much as they used to, and I don't know the last time we did something together. I'm so confused—I always go along with them! What could I have done to make them mad?

Well, I gotta go. Maybe I'll call some of the girls and see if they want to go bowling. I don't really like to bowl—but they all like to, so I guess I'll suggest it.

Or maybe I'll see if Laura's around . . .

# A Monologue About
# Courage

**Frog**  Yeah, hi, get a good look at me. I'm a frog. A greeny-brown, gross frog who lives in the mud and eats flies and other disgusting bugs and never EVER gets a hamburger or tacos or chips.

I've got a story to tell you, so you won't be stupid like me. Here it is. It's not pretty.

I've always been a frog—I mean, I started out as a tadpole, all little and cute, and then swam around, grew some legs—see? *(holds up a leg)* Then I started hopping around with other frogs my age and even flirting with girl frogs, if you know what I mean. See, I may look pretty bad to you, because you're a human being or whatever, but as frogs go, I wasn't too bad off in the looks department.

So one Saturday night, a bunch of us were down by this pond, just hanging around and talking, when these older frogs start hanging with us. They had something they wanted us to try. It was magic, they said. It was some stuff you were supposed to drink and some stuff you were supposed to swallow down real fast, you know, like it was a fly that wasn't quite dead yet. Oh, sorry—I guess that wasn't really very "people-friendly," was it? Anyway, we told these guys to get lost, to go pick on somebody their own size.

But they didn't leave. They told us that this stuff was like serious magic. That if you took it, or drank enough of it, you would turn into— whatever you wanted to be. If you liked being a frog, you would still be a frog, but really good looking and with a great loud low voice. The frog babes would think you were just terrific, and all the other frogs would look up to you. We still told them to beat it, get outta there, leave us alone, you know.

But a couple of us were starting to pay attention . . . just a little bit.

The big frogs talked on and on. They said that if you kept on taking this magic stuff, you could eventually turn into something completely different, and much cooler than a frog! You could be a bigger, stronger animal like the owls that try to swoop down and make snacks out of us every night. And—here's where it got weird—you could turn into something really outrageous, like a human being.

Somebody made a joke about turning into a handsome prince, you know, like who do we have to kiss?—but they acted real serious. They said, "Come on, try a little. One time won't hurt ya. See how it feels! See how much smarter, cooler, and better looking you are. Come on— you'll like it."

*(sighs)*

I really hate to tell you this part. A few of my friends started to say that maybe we should try it. I didn't want to. I thought it sounded stupid, and maybe even dangerous. But my friends kept on pestering me. "Aw, come on," they said. "What can it hurt? It'll be fun!"

I still didn't want to. I guess I was a little scared to try it. But—and this is the worse part—I was more scared to say no to my friends. I felt like they would think I was a coward, or a goody-goody frog. So I gave in. I let them talk me into giving it a try. That night . . . and the next night . . . and the next night after that.

I have to admit, it was fun at first. We did feel different when we took it. We did feel cooler and funnier and like we were better looking. We laughed more than usual, and acted a little crazier, and then laughed some more at each other for acting so crazy. But the

# One Frog's Story

next day we would feel worse, much worse than we had before we started with this "magic" stuff. We wouldn't feel like jumping around, we would just lay in the mud and wait for the big guys to show up and give us some more. But we took it every night, because we were still waiting. We were waiting to turn into owls, and big scary dogs, and six-foot tall human men who lived in houses and drove convertibles. But guess what? Never happened.

We were still frogs—only now we felt like we had been run over by cars and left for frog jerky on the side of the road.

So we finally wised up and told the big frogs to take their show on the road. They said "Well, OK, we'll be seeing you, have a nice life" and stuff, and they left us alone.

Well, my friends and I felt really bad for a few days—and stupid, like who did we think we were kidding? Magic juice and things to swallow that would turn us into other, cooler things? On what planet? We talked about it a lot for a while—we said things like "Those guys were liars!" and "We ought to go sue them or something!" But finally we realized that we were the ones who were stupid, we were the ones who had made the decision to try something so dumb. I was especially a goober—I hadn't even wanted to do it in the first place, but was too scared to do what I knew was right.

But no matter what—we were still undeniably, one hundred per cent, "ribbit"-saying frogs. Nothing we ate or drank turned a single one of us into anything—except stupid.

Thanks for your time.

Now don't be dumb like us.

# Joy Goodheart and the Mustache Melodrama

## A Melodrama About Joyfulness . . . and Citizenship . . . and Other Good Virtues

# Joy Goodheart and the Mustache Melodrama

## CAST

**Snidely Mustache,** *a villain*

**Rip Off Van Winkle,** *Snidely's sidekick*

**Joy Goodheart,** *the heroine*

**Grant Goodheart,** *Joy's father*

**Cal Culator,** *Grant's bookkeeper at The Mill*

**Heartthrob Harry**

**Laura,** *Heartthrob Harry's mother*

**Sally the Shoeshine Girl**

**The Postman**

**A Teacher**

**The Grocer**

**Other People of the Town**

**Wanda**

**Samantha**

**Popcorn Wranglers**

# Joy Goodheart and the Mustache Melodrama

## Notes to the Teacher/Director

OK, OK, so this is mostly just fun and silly and an excuse to throw popcorn. Do you need a fund-raiser for school or other organization? Why not have a family evening of dinner theatre, with a spaghetti dinner first, then this melodrama following the dinner? Find someone who works for a movie theatre or other vendor of popcorn by the bag—you'll need lots of it to throw at the villain, Snidely Mustache.

Though *Joy Goodheart and the Mustache Melodrama* is extremely light-hearted and full of puns, there actually are some values tucked in between the pages. The first value is the idea of joyfulness. We are surrounded by glorious treasures in our lives—our loved ones, beautiful things to see, hear, and smell in nature, and comforts which we take for granted, like a warm home and lots to eat. When Snidely Mustache threatens to remove all the joy from Grant Goodheart's life, Goodheart says that is not possible—he has too much appreciation for the miracles around him. Even his daughter Joy (when tied to the railroad track . . . ) says that if something should happen to her, her father would be very sad for a while, but would not live a joyless life. Well—it would be "Joy-less" but not joyless.

In addition, and in the spirit of a well-known holiday movie, Sally the Shoeshine Girl moves at light speed to collect money from the townspeople, in order to free Grant Goodheart from Snidely Mustache's evil grip. Though treated light-heartedly, it does call to mind the way communities can rally when a child is ill and needs transplant money, for instance, or if a family is displaced by a fire. The spirit of citizenship needs to be encouraged in today's world, extending from school to city to state and country—and indeed global citizenship as we work toward conservation and planet-saving. Wow! We went pretty far afield from Snidely Mustache!

If there is a third value treated in this two-act melodrama, it must surely be that of maintaining a sense of humor. Most of life's problems can best be handled with a stiff upper lip that curls up into a smile. If we can laugh at things, we can work through them. Hopefully, some laughs are built into this fast-moving train, leaving Boston at 5:47 p.m., moving at a speed of . . .

When the actors whisper "Sassa frassa sassa frassa," they are using those nonsense syllables to represent the sounds of people whispering. It should become a little bit clearer as the play goes on, until the final time someone says it, the audience should plainly be able to hear "sassa frassa sassa frassa", for silliness and laughs.

# Joy Goodheart
# and the Mustache Melodrama

## Scenery

To stage this play, you'll need an area designated as the Goodhearts' home, which can stay in place throughout, if your acting area is large enough. All you really must have are two chairs for the Goodhearts, but anything else you can add to create the home atmosphere is encouraged. You might include a portrait of Daisy Goodheart, the departed mom, a table with a bouquet of flowers, etc. (The first time we see Joy, she is winding yarn around her fathers' hands; it might be fun to gather up all of the afghans and other knitted items you can find and position them around your set, giving the idea that Joy has knitted all of them.) The second scene, which could be far stage left, or even in a different part of your performance area (especially if you're in a cafeteria), is the home of Heartthrob Harry and his mother Laura. This is a brief scene which takes place in the kitchen. A counter or desk and a couple of stools should do it—and you'll need a few props. *(See PROPS list.)*

An intermission is built into this play mainly so that, if you're putting on the production as part of a fund-raiser, you can sell sodas and snacks again during the intermission and make a little more money. It will also come in handy, though, if you wish to completely strike the Goodheart house and set the train station. A ladder makes an excellent railroad track or, of course, you can make a track out of construction paper and/or cardboard. You might want to have a little fun with the idea of a train station—in Dallas, the train is called the DART (Dallas Area Rapid Transit); in Chicago, it is called the "L" for elevated train. If your town has a local train, you might want to make a big sign out of butcher paper, or use chalk if you're in a classroom, to create the outside of the station house, using your local train.

If possible, find a recording of a train whistle which can be played more and more loudly, as the train draws near. This should be easily found on a sound effects record, or you can find a whistle which sounds similar to a train whistle, and blow it more and more loudly as the train draws near. The recorded sound of a church bell ringing is also needed, but could also be replaced by a hand-held bell ringing offstage if sound equipment is not available.

# Joy Goodheart and the Mustache Melodrama

## Costumes

For costumes, you could do the play in modern dress and have Snidely Mustache in a business suit (with a raincoat as a cape), but it sure would be fun to go with traditional melodrama attire. Snidely Mustache will need to be dressed all in black with a black cape. It would be great if he could have a tall black hat; it can be rented from a costume store. (Some tuxedo rental places rent hats also—they might trade a rental for an ad in the program?)

Rip Off Van Winkle is unoriginal, ripping off or stealing lines from movies, plays, and commercials; his clothing should be unoriginal as well. What does that mean to your cast? He could be dressed in an exact replica of Snidely's costume. He could have ripped off designer labels showing on all his clothes. With a little creativity, Rip Off Van Winkle's costume can be really clever.

Joy Goodheart needs a long dress with lots of ruffles—pink, white, or yellow, a shawl and some ribbons in her hair.

For the men, you can visit a costume store and see what they have from the melodrama era, or you can suggest the time period by sewing tails on a Salvation Army jacket or by making spats for all the men out of white vinyl. Disposable table clothes are a good source. Glue them in place and add black buttons and fit them down over a black pair of shoes. Cal's outfit can have pencils and pens sticking out of all the pockets, maybe adding machine tape hanging out of his back pocket.

Heartthrob Harry needs to wear a boy scout uniform! One can surely be borrowed in your actor's size, since they are made large enough to accommodate troop leaders. You might want to gray Harry's temples a little, since he is supposed to be 35 years old, or change the line to a slightly younger age. His mom should also wear a long skirt, perhaps with an apron and many pockets for notes and pencils.

*Character Education Book of Plays*
*Middle Grade Level*

# Joy Goodheart
# and the Mustache Melodrama

Sally the Shoeshine Girl can be dressed simply in a long skirt and blouse. She could have an apron with many pockets for rags and shoe polish.

The Postman should have a blue postal worker's uniform (or as close as you can get—white shirt and dark pants should work) with a big shoulder strap bag. (You could attach a stuffed dog to the back of his pants leg as though it is biting our friendly mailman.)

The Schoolteacher should be stereotypical, with wire-rimmed glasses, a bun, high-necked dress with a cameo, and baby-powder-dusted hair. She could carry a ruler or an apple.

The Grocer could have a white shirt with black elastic bands around the upper arms, a big apron, and dark pants. Maybe he has a stalk of celery sticking out of a pocket, or a rubber chicken. (This is one play in which the old saying "Less is more" does not apply!)

The people of the town can wear whatever clothing of the period they would like to wear—long skirts, saloon attire, moms carrying babies (dolls), school children with big lollipops. Wanda and Samantha should enter wearing their school athletic uniforms, or t-shirts and shorts if uniforms are not available.

The Popcorn Wranglers can be dressed in period attire, too, or western wear (since they're wranglers). They are not actually part of the story, so they can be dressed in whatever manner you think would be fun.

# Joy Goodheart
# and the Mustache Melodrama

## Props

Here's the PROP LIST:

- Lots of popcorn (not exactly a prop, but crucial to the production) You may wish, as the script indicates, to put it in small lunch bags with "Throw at villain" written on the side, perhaps decorated with a construction paper mustache. Have the Popcorn Wranglers hand it out at the beginning of the show or you can print programs on one or two sheets of paper and glue to the popcorn bags.

- Yarn for Joy to wind around her father's hands

- A strip of adding machine/calculator tape for Cal

- One piece of popcorn for Rip Off's ear

- Kitchen props for Heartthrob Harry and his mother's kitchen, including:
  Cookbooks
  Notepad
  Pencil

- S'more ingredients for Heartthrob Harry, including:
  Marshmallows
  A chocolate bar
  Graham crackers

- A shoeshine stand for Sally (can be a cardboard box with "Shoeshine Stand" written on it)

- Pencil and paper for Cal

- Ropes to tie Joy to the ladder (railroad track)

# Joy Goodheart and the Mustache Melodrama

## A Melodrama About Joyfulness . . . and Citizenship . . . and Other Good Virtues

# Act 1

## Scene 1

*(As the play begins, the audience sees only a living room set. There are straight-back chairs, a desk, perhaps a fireplace with a picture of dear departed Mom over it. After a moment, SNIDELY MUSTACHE, a villain, enters and addresses the audience with an evil laugh.)*

**Snidely Mustache**   Hooo hooo haaa haaaa! Hello, ladies and gentlemen, and welcome to our play, Joy Goodheart and the Mustache Melodrama! *(as he says 'mustache' he twirls his)* The name is Snidely—Snidely Mustache, evil villain, landlord, and part-time IRS worker—at your service! *(bowing low and brandishing his cape)* Now, before the play begins, I want to discuss something with you. Someone may have already given you a bag of popcorn with an annoying message on it such as "Throw this at villain." I want to tell you right now—that is just rubbish. Throwing popcorn does NOT do anything! It does not make me vanish, it does not make me stop torturing any beautiful girls, it does not make me turn nice in

# Joy Goodheart and the Mustache Melodrama

ANY WAY! SO DON'T THROW POPCORN AT ME, DO YOU HEAR?! *(regaining composure)* Sorry—didn't mean to raise my voice—it's just that I HATE greasy, disgusting, salty, slimy popcorn and it just makes a mess that someone has to sweep up at the end of the night, now doesn't it? So don't throw it! All right—now that we have that out of the way, let me introduce you to my assistant, Rip Off Van Winkle.

*(Enter RIP OFF VAN WINKLE)*

**Rip Off Van Winkle**  Hey, everybody—how ya doin'?

**Snidely Mustache**  Rip Off is my partner in crime, my helper, my administrative assistant.

**Rip Off Van Winkle**  But I don't make coffee.

**Snidely Mustache**  He's a valuable helper, but, well, he's not the most original fellow I've ever known.

**Rip Off Van Winkle**  Are you talking to me?

**Snidely Mustache**  See what I mean?

**Rip Off Van Winkle**  You like me, you really like me!

**Snidely Mustache**  Well, you work cheap. Anyway, this living room belongs to Grant Goodheart—*(pantomimes spitting)* yuck, pooey—and his annoying sweet daughter, Joy Goodheart.

*(Enter GRANT and JOY GOODHEART. They sit facing each other in straight-back chairs. JOY produces a ball of yarn, and her father holds his hands out for her to wrap the yarn around, back and forth from one hand to the other until the yarn is in a rectangle shape.)*

They make me want to drink every drop of Pepto-Bismol in the United States.

# Joy Goodheart and the Mustache Melodrama

| | |
|---|---|
| **Rip Off Van Winkle** | Aw, come on, Snidely. You're just jealous because they're happy all the time and you never are! |
| **Snidely Mustache** | What do you mean, Rip Off? I'm happy whenever I can extort money out of someone, or have the opportunity to step on a bug and squish it flat! |
| **Rip Off Van Winkle** | It's true you do enjoy those things. But you've never forgiven Grant Goodheart for stealing your girlfriend, years ago! |
| **Snidely Mustache** | I told you never to speak of that! |
| **Rip Off Van Winkle** | Yeah, but you told the audience not to throw popcorn, too—let's see how that turns out! |
| **Snidely Mustache** | Enough! Let's exit and let the play get started! |
| **Rip Off Van Winkle** | On with the show, this is it! *(singing)* Overture! Curtain, lights! This is it . . . |
| **Snidely Mustache** | Stop it, Rip Off! I'll be sued! |
| **Rip Off Van Winkle** | *(as they exit)* By a rabbit? |
| **Joy Goodheart** | Oh, Father—life is so good, isn't it? |
| **Grant Goodheart** | Yes it is, my darling daughter Joy. But—what makes you say so today? |
| **Joy Goodheart** | Oh, I don't know—just everything. I have a little crush on someone—it's a beautiful spring day—the flowers are all in bloom—and things are going so well for you at The Mill! |
| **Grant Goodheart** | Yes, I am very fortunate. The Mill is operating successfully, after all these years. I have many loyal employees, and I am indeed a lucky man. |

*Character Education Book of Plays*
*Middle Grade Level*

# Joy Goodheart and the Mustache Melodrama

**Joy Goodheart**    Father—I've always wanted to ask: What do you make at The Mill?

**Grant Goodheart**    You know, Joy—I have no idea. But it's running smoothly!

**Joy Goodheart**    That's the important thing.

**Grant Goodheart**    No—the important thing is that I have such a beautiful daughter, with such a sunny disposition and a kind heart. My only regret is—

**Joy Goodheart**    Father! You have a regret, on such a perfect day? Whatever could it be?

**Grant Goodheart**    Only that your mother, the fair Daisy, couldn't be here to see the lovely young woman you have become.

**Joy Goodheart**    Oh, yes, that. By the way, father . . . why isn't my mother here?

**Grant Goodheart**    Not enough girls tried out for the play.

**Joy Goodheart**    That's right. Now I remember.

**Grant Goodheart**    Joy, dear—whatever are you going to do with all this yarn?

**Joy Goodheart**    Oh Father, I haven't a clue! But wrapping it around your hands is such a wholesome-looking activity!

**Grant Goodheart**    Indeed it is.

*(Enter CAL CULATOR, carrying a long strip of adding machine tape and looking very frightened.)*

# Joy Goodheart
# and the Mustache Melodrama

**Cal Culator**    Excuse me . . . Mr. Goodheart? Oh, hello, Joy.

**Joy Goodheart**    Hello, Mr. Culator.

**Grant Goodheart**    Oh, Joy—I didn't realize you'd met my accountant, Cal.

**Joy Goodheart**    Of course! I've known Mr. Cal Culator for years!

**Cal Culator**    I'm so sorry to interrupt, Mr. Goodheart, but something's terribly wrong. It's about our agreement with the landlord, Snidely Mustache.

**Grant Goodheart**    Do you mean our agreement not to paint The Mill without letting him choose the colors?

**Cal Culator**    No, the other one.

**Grant Goodheart**    No pets on the premises?

**Cal Culator**    No, sir. I mean the fact that we agreed to pay him forty percent of the profit we make selling . . . whatever it is we make at The Mill!

**Grant Goodheart**    Oh yes, I'm familiar with that agreement.

**Cal Culator**    Well, there's been a terrible mistake. Someone . . . that is . . . I . . . misfigured—it's hard to explain, but basically we owe Mr. Mustache *(whispering into GRANT's ear)* sassa frassa sassa frassa!

**Grant Goodheart**    We owe him how much?

**Cal Culator**    *(whispering into his ear again)* Sassa frassa sassa frassa!

**Grant Goodheart**    That's a huge amount! How could a mistake like this have happened?

# Joy Goodheart and the Mustache Melodrama

**Cal Culator**    Well, I never told you this, sir, but I didn't complete Pre-Algebra, Algebra, Geometry and Calc! I only had "Arithmetic!"

**Grant Goodheart**    So this is how I find out.

**Cal Culator**    I'll make it up to you somehow, sir! I promise!

*(While GRANT GOODHEART, JOY GOODHEART and CAL CULATOR huddle together to look at the adding machine tape, SNIDELY MUSTACHE and RIP OFF VAN WINKLE enter and pantomime listening in at the GOODHEARTS' living room door. The audience throws popcorn at SNIDELY.)*

**Snidely Mustache**    All right, all right, that's enough! Stop it right now! I'm trying to eavesdrop and you'll give me away!

**Rip Off Van Winkle**    I can't hear what they're saying! I'm trying but . . . *(SNIDELY pulls a piece of popcorn out of RIP OFF's ear)* Hey, that's better! *(singing)* I can hear clearly now, the popcorn's gone!

**Grant Goodheart**    Whatever are we going to do? We owe this money to Snidely Mustache fair and square—but how will we ever raise it?

**Joy Goodheart**    I could sell my porcelain doll collection!

**Grant Goodheart**    Your mother left you that, child! I can't allow it.

**Cal Culator**    It's all my fault. Dock my pay. I'll work for free for . . . five years . . . no, six . . . *(tries to figure the amount, becomes upset)* . . . I can't figure it out! I'm a complete failure as an accountant!

**Grant Goodheart**    There there, Cal. Somehow we'll get the money that we owe Snidely Mustache.

# Joy Goodheart
# and the Mustache Melodrama

| | |
|---|---|
| **Snidely Mustache** | *(boldly entering the GOODHEARTS' living room)* Grant Goodheart! Hello! Did I hear my name in the same sentence with the words "money that we owe"? |
| **Grant Goodheart** | Yes, Mr. Mustache, I'm afraid there's been an accounting error at The Mill. *(CAL CULATOR turns his back in shame and JOY comforts him)* We haven't been paying you enough—we owe you *(whispering)* sassa frassa sassa frassa! |
| **Snidely Mustache** | Did you say *(also whispering)* sassa frassa sassa frassa? |
| **Grant Goodheart** | I'm afraid I did. |
| **Snidely Mustache** | Delicious! |
| **Rip Off Van Winkle** | How much does he owe? |
| **Snidely Mustache** | *(whispering to RIP OFF)* Sassa frassa sassa frassa! |
| **Rip Off Van Winkle** | *(falls down in shock)* I've fallen and I can't get up! |
| **Snidely Mustache** | *(ignoring RIP OFF)* Well, this is an interesting situation, Mr. Goodheart! This money is rightfully mine, as I'm sure you agree . . . |
| **Grant Goodheart** | Yes, Mr. Mustache, I quite agree. |
| **Snidely Mustache** | And you also must realize that I'm entitled to interest because this money should have been mine all along . . . |
| **Grant Goodheart** | Surely you intend to be reasonable . . . |

*Character Education Book of Plays*
*Middle Grade Level*

# Joy Goodheart and the Mustache Melodrama

**Snidely Mustache** — Were you reasonable when you cheated me out of money that was owed me? Were you reasonable when you stole Daisy, the love of my life . . . oops, I mean . . . when you didn't make the proper payments?

**Grant Goodheart** — I'm sure we can come to some terms!

**Snidely Mustache** — The only terms I will come to with you will be a prison term!

**Rip Off Van Winkle** — *(rising)* How about a term of endearment?

**Snidely Mustache** — You'll pay me every penny of the money you owe me . . . plus interest at 8.125% . . .

**Cal Culator** — I've never known how to figure interest. Do you multiply the big number times "point 08125" or "8 point 125"?

**Snidely Mustache** — I suggest you do the math yourself, Goodheart. Because I expect it in full by the end of the business day today.

**Grant Goodheart** — Today?!

**Cal Culator** — Today?!

**Snidely Mustache** — Today.

**Rip Off Van Winkle** — Couldn't you give them until tomorrow? Then I could sing *(singing)* Tomorrow! Tomorrow! I love ya—tomorrow!

**Snidely Mustache** — No, today. And if I don't have it by close of business, why, I'll . . . I'll . . . I'll steal the joy out of your life!

**Grant Goodheart** — Mustache! What do you mean? My daughter Joy—or all the happiness I enjoy on a day-to-day basis?

# Joy Goodheart
# and the Mustache Melodrama

**Snidely Mustache**   I guess you'll find out at five o'clock, eh Goodheart?! Come on, Rip Off! We've got some financial planning to do.

**Rip Off Van Winkle**   Who wants to be a millionaire?

**Snidely Mustache**   I do, Rip Off—and I'm well on my way!

**Rip Off Van Winkle**   Is that your final answer?

**Snidely Mustache**   Yes! Now, come on!

*(As RIP OFF VAN WINKLE and SNIDELY MUSTACHE exit, the GOODHEARTS and CAL CULATOR begin to console each other silently, patting each other on the back and pacing a bit. RIP OFF VAN WINKLE and SNIDELY MUSTACHE pause outside the front door.)*

**Snidely Mustache**   What Grant Goodheart doesn't know, Rip Off, is that I am the sneakiest landlord in town! I have been creeping into his office for years and replacing the batteries in his accountant's calculator with "brand X" batteries! Their math has been wrong for a long time! And they didn't notice 'til now!

**Rip Off Van Winkle**   What a great idea, Boss! The math errors just keep *(pantomiming a big pink bunny beating a drum)* going . . . and going . . . and going . . .

**Snidely Mustache**   Yes, that's what's happened! He really doesn't owe me any more money, but he'll never figure that out! Now I'm in a "win-win" situation—if he gets the money, I'm rich beyond my wildest dreams—and if he doesn't, I'll be able finally to ruin his life! Now, let's scram—I need to open some Swiss bank accounts! *(looks at the audience)* Don't even think about it!

*(They exit, as SNIDELY laughs in an evil manner.)*

*Character Education Book of Plays*
*Middle Grade Level*

# Joy Goodheart
# and the Mustache Melodrama

## Scene 2

*(This scene takes place in the home of HEARTTHROB HARRY and his mother, LAURA. HEARTTHROB HARRY, though a good-looking heartthrob, is the world's oldest Boy Scout. He is in his mother's kitchen, helping her prepare the family's menu for the week.)*

**Laura**   Heartthrob Harry, it's so nice of you to help me plan the family's menu for the week! It's very hard to think of interesting things to cook on a budget!

**Heartthrob Harry**   You're welcome, Mom. Don't forget—part of my Family Member badge is to help plan the menu for at least one night! Do we have a green vegetable for Wednesday? *(LAURA starts to lift a heavy cookbook)* Here—let me help you with that cookbook! It looks heavy.

**Laura**   You're such a good boy, Heartthrob Harry. I'm so lucky to have a thirty-five year old Boy Scout in the family! You're so helpful!

**Heartthrob Harry**   Well, Mom, as you well know—I'm going to stay in Boy Scouts until I advance to Eagle Scout, no matter how long it takes. So far I'm only a few badges short.

**Laura**   Lucky me!

**Heartthrob Harry**   Something's troubling me today, Mom.

**Laura**   What on earth? Tell Mommy all about it! After all—I am my kid's mom!

**Heartthrob Harry**   Well . . . I've met this girl. Or I should say, a young lady.

**Laura**   I knew this day would come . . .

**Heartthrob Harry**   I was helping people cross the street in front of The Mill—

# Joy Goodheart
# and the Mustache Melodrama

when I saw her. She was as beautiful as a sunset—as tender as a newborn calf—as delicate as a rosebud.

**Laura** What a beautiful description!

**Heartthrob Harry** Thanks—I'm working on my "Poet" badge.

**Laura** You might want to leave out the "newborn calf" part. Not too many woman want to be compared to a cow of any age, even a little calf.

**Heartthrob Harry** OK. Anyway, our eyes met and I knew I wanted to ask her to marry me—or at least to the movies—but then an old lady came along and I had to help her across the street. When I looked around—the beautiful young woman was gone!

**Laura** Do you have any idea who she is?

**Heartthrob Harry** Yes—I think she may be Joy Goodheart, daughter of Grant Goodheart, The Mill's owner!

**Laura** Oh yes, I know Joy Goodheart! She belongs to my yarn-winding club! I could introduce you!

**Heartthrob Harry** Thanks, Mom—but I'm timid! I'm afraid she won't want to be courted by the world's oldest Boy Scout! What if she thinks I'm—you know—corny! Or squirrely! Or insane!

**Laura** Don't be silly, darling! What woman doesn't want a man who's courteous and brave, looks good in a uniform, and knows how to plan a menu?! Go over there right now and ask that girl out on a date! Here's the address! *(she writes a note and gives it to HEARTTHROB HARRY)*

**Heartthrob Harry** Thanks, Mom! I'll be back in time to help plan dessert!

*(HEARTTHROB HARRY exits excitedly, and LAURA and POPCORN WRANGLERS strike the kitchen set and exit.)*

# Joy Goodheart
# and the Mustache Melodrama

# Scene 3

*(Meanwhile, back at the GOODHEARTS' house . . . CAL CULATOR, GRANT and JOY GOOD-HEART are trying to decide how to raise the money.)*

| | |
|---|---|
| **Cal Culator** | It's impossible, Mr. Goodheart! There's no way we can raise that kind of money by five o'clock. |
| **Grant Goodheart** | We could go to the bank! Take out a loan! |
| **Cal Culator** | Are you kidding? It's after three. There's not a banker at his desk. |
| **Grant Goodheart** | You're right. |
| **Joy Goodheart** | We could have a bake sale! I could make my famous blueberry muffins! |
| **Grant Goodheart** | Joy, you're the sweetest girl in town. But there's no time! We'd have to sell muffins for thousands of dollars a piece! |
| **Joy Goodheart** | We could sell them in Highland Park! *(insert the wealthy part of your town, or gated community)* |
| **Grant Goodheart** | Thank you, but I don't think that will work. Drat that Mustache—why must he be so unfair! It was an honest math error! |
| **Cal Culator** | Only an evil landlord would threaten to steal all the joy out of a man's life. What a substantial penalty! |
| **Grant Goodheart** | You know, Cal, Joy—the truth is, he can't. There is so much joy in my life—he can't possibly remove it all! Why, I get a tear in my eye when I look out the window and see the seasons change! I was married to a wonderful woman and |

# Joy Goodheart
# and the Mustache Melodrama

although she is no longer with us, the memory of our time together fills my heart to overflowing with fond happiness. I have good friends here in town, a thriving business, a comfortable home—I love books and music, and the occasional fishing trip down at Beaver Creek Pond. And the fact that I have this beautiful, sweet daughter is more than I deserve. So come on, Snidely Mustache! Come ahead! You can't possibly take the joy from my rich, full life!

*(A knock at the door—all characters jump as if startled)*

**Grant Goodheart**   Well, I didn't mean right now!

*(He goes to the door and it is not SNIDELY, but HEARTTHROB HARRY.)*

**Grant Goodheart**   Yes? May I help you?

**Heartthrob Harry**   Yes, Mr. Goodheart. My name is Heartthrob Harry, and, if I may, I'd like to see your daughter Joy.

*(JOY has seen who it is and has run up behind her father)*

**Joy Goodheart**   Hello! I was hoping I would see you again!

**Heartthrob Harry**   Really? I mean—you remember me?

**Grant Goodheart**   Come in, son, come in. Any heartthrob of my daughter's is a heartthrob of . . . that is to say . . . is welcome in my home. We're not at our best, I'm afraid—we've just found out we owe our landlord a great deal of money by five o'clock today!

**Heartthrob Harry**   *(crossing to stand by JOY)* Really? How can I help?

**Cal Culator**   No one can help; we're doomed!

**Grant Goodheart**   Harry, I can't help noticing that you seem to be a . . . that is, a Boy Scout.

# Joy Goodheart and the Mustache Melodrama

**Heartthrob Harry**  Yes, sir, I am. I think I'm pretty much the oldest living Boy Scout, determined to get all my badges and progress to Eagle Scout.

**Grant Goodheart**  I was a Scout myself. Ever make a s'more?

**Heartthrob Harry**  Did I ever make a s'more?! You bet 'cha! *(reaches in his pocket and pulls out marshmallows, a chocolate bar and a couple of Graham crackers)* I could make one right now, if you like!

**Cal Culator**  You have s'more ingredients in your pocket?

**Heartthrob Harry**  Well . . . always prepared . . .

**Joy Goodheart**  I think a s'more sounds like just the thing to take our minds off of our troubles!

**Grant Goodheart**  You might be right, Joy. Not much is more delicious and uplifting than a s'more. But I've always wondered—do you melt the marshmallow first and let that melt the chocolate? Or do you melt the chocolate too, somehow? I can't figure out now to get it on the straightened-out coat hanger!

**Heartthrob Harry**  Well, come on! Let's go into your kitchen and I'll assemble and cook a s'more for each of us!

**Grant Goodheart**  *(as they exit offstage to the "kitchen")* Sounds great. Now let me see—did you select regular marshmallows or minis?

*(another knock at the door)*

**Joy Goodheart**  You just keep impressing . . . I mean, getting to know my father, Heartthrob Harry—I'll see who's at the door.

# Joy Goodheart
# and the Mustache Melodrama

*(She crosses to the door and opens it. SNIDELY MUSTACHE is there, but has his cape pulled up over his head and speaks in an old lady voice. RIP OFF VAN WINKLE is at the far edge of the stage, making whimpering puppy sounds.)*

**Joy Goodheart**   Yes? May I help you?

**Snidely Mustache**   Yes, dear, I hope so. My little puppy seems to have been hurt somehow—I don't know how, but he's limping terribly! Hear him? *(RIP OFF VAN WINKLE really begins to howl)* He's in such dreadful pain—but I'm sure he's going to be in much worse pain in a minute! *(he simmers down)* Won't you come have a look at him!

**Joy Goodheart**   A little puppy! Of course! I'll come right away! *(exiting with SNIDELY MUSTACHE)* Where is he? Take me to him at once!

**Snidely Mustache**   *(dropping the fake voice)* I'll take you somewhere, my dear, but it won't be to see any puppy!

**Joy Goodheart**   Snidely Mustache!

**Snidely Mustache**   Yes, Little Missy, that's right! Your father's not going to have that money by five o'clock—so I'll have his Joy as a down payment! Come on! *(grabs her arm and pulls her off stage)*

**Joy Goodheart**   Father! Heartthrob Harry! Cal! Help! HELP!

*(GRANT GOODHEART, HEARTTHROB HARRY and CAL CULATOR re-enter, not noticing JOY GOODHEART's disappearance. They are all chewing, pantomiming finishing s'mores. )*

**Heartthrob Harry**   And that's how you make the perfect s'more!

**Grant Goodheart**   Excellent—oh wait! We didn't make one for Joy. *(looking around for her)* Joy?

**Cal Culator**   She was here just a minute ago! Making eyes at Heartthrob Harry!

# Joy Goodheart and the Mustache Melodrama

**Heartthrob Harry**   Was she really? Or are you just saying that . . . ?

**Cal Culator**   No, I mean it! She really had those little imaginary cartoon hearts popping all around her head!

**Heartthrob Harry**   Wow.

**Grant Goodheart**   Good heavens, where is she? Joy! Joy, where are you?!

**Cal Culator**   Miss Goodheart! Joy!

**Heartthrob Harry**   Joy!

*(another knock at the door)*

**Grant Goodheart**   Ahhh! Perhaps she locked herself out. *(crosses to front door and opens it. It is not JOY, but SALLY THE SHOESHINE GIRL)* Sally the Shoeshine Girl! What are you doing here?

**Sally the Shoeshine Girl**   Well, Mr. Goodheart, pardon me for coming to your house, but I thought you'd want to know. I just came from the train station where I work, you know, shining shoes? And Snidely Mustache has your daughter, Joy—I mean, I know you know your daughter's name, but I thought you might have more than one—anyway, your daughter whose name is Joy is there with Mustache. And I hate to tell you this—but he's tied her to the railroad track!

**Grant Goodheart**   No!

**Heartthrob Harry**   This can't be happening! I've just met the girl of my dreams—and now she's about to be turned into a fruit roll-up!

**Cal Culator**   It's all my fault, Sally. Because of a math error I made, the company owes Mr. Mustache *(whispering)* sassa frassa sassa

# Joy Goodheart and the Mustache Melodrama

|   |   |
|---|---|
| | frassa *(speaking regularly)* dollars! We're supposed to raise the money by five o'clock— |
| **Grant Goodheart** | Or he's going to steal the joy out of my life! |
| **Sally the Shoeshine Girl** | I'd say he jumped the gun a little! How much money did you say? |
| **Cal Culator** | *(again, whispering in SALLY'S ear)* Sassa frassa, sassa frassa. |
| **Sally the Shoeshine Girl** | That's a lot . . . and yet . . . |
| **Cal Culator** | *(interrupting her)* Sally, when does the next train arrive? |
| **Sally the Shoeshine Girl** | You know, Cal, I was trying to figure that out. See, one train left New Orleans at 2:20 p.m., traveling at a rate of 60 miles per hour. Another one left Little Rock at 1:30 p.m., traveling at 55 miles per hour. I can't seem to figure out which one will get to the local station first! |
| **Cal Culator** | Wait—this is Arithmetic! It's a word problem! I can do this! *(CAL CULATOR gets paper and pencil and scratches while the others look on eagerly)* We've got fifteen minutes. Let's go! |
| **Heartthrob Harry & Grant Goodheart** | *(ad libbing)* Yeah, come on! No time to lose! *(etc.)* |

*(Everyone exits the same direction except SALLY THE SHOESHINE GIRL who stands there thinking for a moment, then exits the other direction, looking like she has a good idea.)*

|   |   |
|---|---|
| **A Popcorn Wrangler** | Will they get there in time? Will Snidely Mustache make road kill out of Joy Goodheart? Will the train be late—or right on time? Come back after this brief intermission—and all will be revealed! |

*Character Education Book of Plays
Middle Grade Level*

# Joy Goodheart
## and the Mustache Melodrama

# Intermission

# Joy Goodheart
# and the Mustache Melodrama

# Act 2

## The Only Scene in Act 2

*(At the train station. JOY GOODHEART is tied to the "track" and struggling to get free. SNIDELY MUSTACHE paces behind her, obviously enjoying the moment. RIP OFF VAN WINKLE stands by, looking a little worried.)*

**Joy Goodheart**   You'll never get away with this, Mr. Mustache! Never! My father and Heartthrob Harry are on their way right now!

**Snidely Mustache**   Dream on, silly child! They're more interested in chestnuts roasting on an open fire than their precious Joy!

**Rip Off Van Winkle**   There aren't really chestnuts in s'mores are there?

**Snidely Mustache**   No, Rip Off, I was just . . . oh never mind.

**Rip Off Van Winkle**   Snide-Man, this is starting to get creepy. I'm all for fame and fortune, but do we really want to do away with Miss Joy Dishwashing Liquid here? I mean—what if they don't make it on time to rescue her—and the train comes . . .

**Snidely Mustache**   Grant Goodheart has vexed me for the last time, Rip Off! I'm ruining his life once and for all!

**Rip Off Van Winkle**   But Snidely—you don't want to actually—you know --

**Snidely Mustache**   I want to do whatever it takes to bring down Grant Goodheart.

# Joy Goodheart and the Mustache Melodrama

**Rip Off Van Winkle**    Well—I hate to do this. *(turns to the audience)* Do you believe that bad people can turn good? Do you? Well, if you believe that we can turn Snidely Mustache good and get him to free Joy Goodheart—throw your popcorn now! Throw it for all you're worth! That's right! Save his little evil heart!

*(The audience hurls popcorn—RIP OFF looks expectantly at SNIDELY.)*

Well? You gonna set her free?

**Snidely Mustache**    I told you! Popcorn doesn't do anything! Why don't you listen? No, I'm not going to set her free! And now there's a big mess on the floor, just like I said.

**Rip Off Van Winkle**    Oh well, it was worth a shot.

**Joy Goodheart**    Mr. Mustache, don't you see? You can't ruin my father's life. If you kill me, he'll be very sad for a while—but he'll see joy in everything, all around him—a bloom on a rose bush, the first cool breeze of fall, the crest of a wave!

**Snidely Mustache**    No, I refuse to believe it. You are his joy and life without you is no life at all.

**Joy Goodheart**    There's much good in his heart, Mr. Mustache. I'm sorry for your unhappiness—whatever the cause—but you just can't ruin my father's life, no matter what . . .

*(GRANT GOODHEART, HEARTTHROB HARRY and CAL CULATOR enter, breathlessly.)*

**Heartthrob Harry**    Thank goodness! We're not too late!

**Grant Goodheart**    Joy! Are you all right?

**Joy Goodheart**    Yes, father, I'm fine! *(train whistle sound effect is heard)* But maybe you'd better hurry!

# Joy Goodheart
# and the Mustache Melodrama

| | |
|---|---|
| **Snidely Mustache** | Get out of here, Goodheart! You'll never free her in time! The train from . . . let's see, is it Little Rock? . . . anyway, one of the trains is rapidly approaching! |
| **Cal Culator** | Let's get him! |

*(As SNIDELY MUSTACHE tries to run, CAL CULATOR and GRANT GOODHEART stop him, each one grabbing an arm.)*

| | |
|---|---|
| **Grant Goodheart** | You're not going anywhere, Mustache! |
| **Heartthrob Harry** | There'll be an arrest warrant with your name on it down at police headquarters! |

*(another train whistle, louder)*

| | |
|---|---|
| **Joy Goodheart** | Guys? |
| **Snidely Mustache** | The train draws closer and closer and with it the ruin of your pitiful life, Goodheart! |
| **Grant Goodheart** | Oh, Mustache—Daisy didn't leave you for me—she left you because you were evil! She wanted a much less sinister man to marry—one who actually worked for a living and didn't try to kill people all the time! |
| **Snidely Mustache** | So I have a few faults! She left me flat and married you! |
| **Rip Off Van Winkle** | Listen, it's good to get this all out, but I think we better free Joy . . . |
| **Snidely Mustache** | You're outta luck, Goodheart! I strapped her onto that railroad track with some special radioactive cord which I appropriated from the scientist's laboratory last weekend! No one can free her but me! |

*Character Education Book of Plays*
*Middle Grade Level*

# Joy Goodheart and the Mustache Melodrama

**Heartthrob Harry**   What a lot of hooey! I can set her free!

**Cal Culator**   Heartthrob Harry, wait! If he's telling the truth, and those cords are radioactive—you'll be committing suicide!

**Rip Off Van Winkle**   You know, this could've come up in conversation a few hours ago . . .

**Heartthrob Harry**   Who cares? Life without Joy is not worth living. I'll risk all to save her. *(He dives to the task of freeing her, as another train whistle sounds.)*

**Grant Goodheart**   Hurry, Heartthrob Harry, hurry! That train is getting dangerously close!

**Cal Culator**   Mustache—what's the secret? How do you undo those cords?!

**Snidely Mustache**   You'd like to know, wouldn't you? Too bad!

**Rip Off Van Winkle**   Er . . . pardon me, boys—is that the Chattanooga Choo-Choo?

**Heartthrob Harry**   Wait a minute, everybody! He's lying!

**Grant Goodheart**   Who's lying?!

**Heartthrob Harry**   Mustache! This isn't any radioactive cord—it's just rope! He's just tied her down here with knots! *(jumping to his feet and giving a Boy Scout salute)* And I'm a Boy Scout! I know everything there is to know about untying knots! *(he kneels again and, with hands flying at the speed of light, unties the knots and frees JOY, who jumps up)* There! I just earned my Ropes & Knots badge!

**Joy Goodheart**   *(throwing her arms around his neck)* My hero!

# Joy Goodheart
# and the Mustache Melodrama

**Snidely Mustache**   Rats!

**Rip Off Van Winkle**   What a world!

**Grant Goodheart**   *(letting go of SNIDELY and rushing to his daughter.)* Joy!

**Joy Goodheart**   Father!

**Rip Off Van Winkle**   Group hug?

**Grant Goodheart**   Look out, everybody—here comes the train!

*(Everyone follows carefully choreographed head movements as they watch the train turn suddenly and miss them entirely.)*

**Cal Culator**   Hey—what just happened?!

**Heartthrob Harry**   Great—I was hoping it would work. In case I couldn't free Joy, I took a couple of pieces of aluminum foil and attached them to the railroad track. The aluminum shorted out the metal wheels—or something—and made it change course and take the other track out of town!

**Grant Goodheart**   Aluminum foil?

**Rip Off Van Winkle**   Oh oh, don't say it . . .

**Snidely Mustache**   Curses . . . foiled again!

**Rip Off Van Winkle**   Now who's ripping people off! I think that calls for a popcorn pelting!

*(popcorn pelting if there is any left)*

**Joy Goodheart**   Father—Heartthrob Harry—I knew you'd save me!

*Character Education Book of Plays*
*Middle Grade Level*

# Joy Goodheart and the Mustache Melodrama

**Cal Culator**  Thank goodness—but none of this would ever have happened if—

*(enter SALLY THE SHOESHINE GIRL followed by a lot of PEOPLE OF THE TOWN)*

**Sally the Shoeshine Girl**  Mr. Goodheart! Joy! Am I too late?!

**Heartthrob Harry**  Well, Joy is safe, if that's what you mean!

**Sally the Shoeshine Girl**  No, I'm talking about the money that you owe Snidely Mustache!

**Snidely Mustache**  Yeah! What about that! Just because I tied your daughter to a railroad track doesn't mean I'm not entitled to my money!

**Sally the Shoeshine Girl**  Well—when I heard what had happened, I went from door to door, all around the town! All I had to do was mention your name, Mr. Goodheart, and all the neighbors pitched in! Just look! *(she up-ends a big shoeshine stand full of cash)* We raised a total of sassa frassa sassa frassa!

**The Postman**  Why, when the postal workers went on strike, Mr. Goodheart gave me work at The Mill. He put food on my table when we were hungry!

**A Teacher**  When Joy Goodheart was in my fifth grade class, Mr. Goodheart came up and helped me run off copies and collate test pages! I'm in his debt!

**The Grocer**  I work at the Chow Down Food Store, and Mr. Goodheart always returns his cart to the proper place in the parking lot! I'm happy to contribute money for him!

**Grant Goodheart**  I don't know what to say!

*(sound effect of a church bell ringing)*

# Joy Goodheart and the Mustache Melodrama

**Rip Off Van Winkle**    Every time a bell rings, an angel gets his wings!

**Cal Culator**    What does that have to do with anything?

**Rip Off Van Winkle**    Well, nothing, it's just that this scene reminds me of . . . you know, Zuzu's petals . . . oh, forget it.

**Heartthrob Harry**    I think this calls for a song! *(singing)*
SHOULD AULD ACQUAINTANCE BE FORGOT,
AND NEVER BROUGHT TO MIND . . .

**Cast**    *(joining in)* WE'LL TAKE A CUP OF KINDNESS YET . . .

*(enter WANDA and SAMANTHA)*

**Wanda**    Hi—excuse me?

*(everyone stops singing and looks at the newcomers)*

**Samantha**    Yeah, sorry to interrupt—but we can be in the play now!

**Grant Goodheart**    What? Who are you?

**Wanda**    I'm Wanda and this is Samantha. We wanted to try out for the play, but we're in after-school athletics. Anyway, practice is canceled today, and so we can be in the play if you still need girls.

**Grant Goodheart**    Perfect! One of you can play Daisy, my wife!

**Joy Goodheart**    Wait—I've got it! One can play Daisy, my mother, your wife, Dad—

**Samantha**    *(trying to fit into her role, but being a little confused)* Uh—dear! It's so good to see you!

*Character Education Book of Plays*
*Middle Grade Level*

# Joy Goodheart and the Mustache Melodrama

**Joy Goodheart**   That's right! And the other one can play the same part, but she gets to marry Snidely Mustache! See—two woman playing the same part! Both men get to marry one of them—and they don't have to hate each other anymore!

**Rip Off Van Winkle**   Yeah! *(to SNIDELY MUSTACHE)* You don't have to be evil now because you didn't get your true love taken away from you! Here she is!

**Wanda**   Sounds good to me. *(assuming her part)* Here I am darling, after all these years! Ready to make you not be evil anymore!

**Snidely Mustache**   I don't know what to say! I get to marry my Daisy after all?

**Joy Goodheart**   Of course you do! Now will you forgive my dad and let us live in peace?

**Rip Off Van Winkle**   Now there's an offer you can't refuse!

**Snidely Mustache**   Yes! Yes, of course! If Daisy is at my side—well, I cannot tell a lie. This money isn't rightfully mine. It's a long story . . .

**Rip Off Van Winkle**   And I'll be glad to tell it. See, there was this bad battery . . .

**Snidely Mustache**   Suffice it to say, I will immediately return all this money to the good citizens of this town.

**A Teacher**   Wait! Let's don't take back our money! Let's build a recreation center where our children can play!

**The Postman**   Yes! Or a beautiful park!

**The Grocer**   Or a library!

**All**   *(ad libbing)* Great idea! Let's do it! Sounds great! etc.

# Joy Goodheart
# and the Mustache Melodrama

**Grant Goodheart**  My Daisy! How wonderful to see you!

**Snidely Mustache**  My Daisy! How wonderful to see you!

**Wanda and Samantha**  *(in unison)* We're so happy not to have athletics practice.

**Heartthrob Harry**  Will you marry me, Joy? And fill my life with Joy forever?

**Joy Goodheart**  Of course I will! Say! Sally, The Shoeshine Girl . . .

**All**  SALLY THE SHOESHINE GIRL!

**Joy Goodheart**  No, I mean—Say! How can I ever thank you, Sally the Shoeshine Girl?

**Sally the Shoeshine Girl**  Well—I wouldn't mind a date with Cal, here! I love a man who can work long division!

**Cal Culator**  You got it!

**Rip Off Van Winkle**  Hey, are there any more girls? One for me? No—OK, then, I will just say "And they all lived according to their happiest expectations."

**All**  What?

**Rip Off Van Winkle**  From then on, their lives were content and peaceful.

**All**  What?

**Rip Off Van Winkle**  OK, OK. THEY ALL LIVED HAPPILY EVER AFTER!

**Snidely Mustache**  Ladies and gentlemen, now is the time to throw popcorn!

**All**  *(waving)* Good-bye! Thanks for coming!

*Character Education Book of Plays*
*Middle Grade Level*